CHEATERS ALWAYS WIN

The Story of America

J.M. FENSTER

TWELVE

New York Boston

Twelve
Hachette Book Group
1290 Avenue of the Americas, New York, NY 10104
twelvebooks.com
twitter.com/twelvebooks

First Edition: December 2019

Twelve is an imprint of Grand Central Publishing. The Twelve name and logo are trademarks of Hachette Book Group, Inc.

The publisher is not responsible for websites (or their content) that are not owned by the publisher.

The Hachette Speakers Bureau provides a wide range of authors for speaking events. To find out more, go to www.hachettespeakersbureau.com or call (866) 376-6591.

Library of Congress Cataloging-in-Publication Data has been applied for.

ISBNs: 978-1-5387-2870-3 (hardcover), 978-1-5387-3261-8 (ebook)

Book design by Marie Mundaca

Printed in the United States of America

LSC-C

10 9 8 7 6 5 4 3 2 1

For Matt Callaway

George Washington

Charlie Bruckhauser

CONTENTS

INTRODUCTION

What Is Cheating?

When I set out to study cheating, I naturally told everyone I met about my new project and soon found that some people blushed red at the very sound of the word. Then I would blush, it being obvious that the other person had just inadvertently confessed something very intimate. Being a polite American first and an ace investigator second, I'd change the subject as quickly as possible. One colleague to whom I mentioned cheating in the course of conversation still averts her eyes when we meet. It's all part of the uncomfortable excitement that surrounds cheating.

Acquaintances who took the news of my research in a smoother stride would typically ask why I had chosen that particular topic. "Dogs don't cheat!" was my reply. I was so emphatic about this kernel of life experience that I'd repeat it, adding cats and horses: *They* don't cheat. My idea at the start was that humans are the only species that cheats, and because the possibility of it enters into their every endeavor, it's central to the daily trial of being human: whether to cheat or not to cheat.

Dogs, however, don't occupy the narrow space between those twin guide rails; only humans go through life ricocheting back and forth between the two, or else clutching one, while eyeing the other. That's the human lot. And *dogs don't cheat.*

That was before I learned that I was entirely wrong. While still in the talking stage of this book, I played Fetch with my dog, Bisbee, one evening, just as always. He is a creature so pure-hearted that my big joke is that Jesus has a bumper sticker on his car that says, "What would Bisbee do?" I learned all at once that among other things, Bisbee would cheat. On the day in question, he stole the ball and suddenly turned Fetch into a different game, one called Let's-Make-the-Lethargic-Human-Chase-the-Dog-All-Over-the-House. The look on his face was the happiest I'd ever seen. His eyes alive, his tail nearly slapping his sides. He had just realized that he was calling the shots. He didn't have to play Fetch; he had possession of the ball. His face shone with the bright rays of discovery. The first few times Bisbee changed the game, I went along, ever good-natured, and played Chase. On the day that I didn't, staying put and bellowing that he was a goddamned cheater, he ate the ball.

Bisbee's point, which was incisive, was that he hadn't agreed to any particular game or any prevailing rules. My counterargument was that simply by participating in the first game—Fetch—he had tacitly committed to that game, as well as its rules. Between our two views lay the aspect of cheating that is peculiarly human: the expressed acceptance of rules.

In the natural world, the one that embraces all

species, including Bisbee's, rules are only implied. Testing them to push for greater comfort or happiness isn't cheating; it's behavioral evolution, a certain sign of life.

Humans may not be the only creatures to make up rules, but they are unquestionably the only ones who expect someone else to commit voluntarily and in advance to following them, preferably in writing. People take wedding vows—nobody makes them do that. They sign honor codes, though they will not starve to death if they don't. They enter into contracts to play sports, but only if they choose to. Some commitments may be slightly less explicit, but they are no less definite.

Ironically enough, agreeing to be bound constitutes the ultimate proof that a human is free. Consenting to follow a certain set of rules—voluntarily—is an act of self-determination. When enslaved or bound in fiefdom, forced into an arranged marriage or strong-armed into a religious sect, a person cannot cheat. It isn't possible. They might "behaviorally evolve," but they can't betray rules to which they didn't agree. They cannot cheat in the sense of interest to this book. Looking on the positive side of miserable circumstances, one cannot be a slimy, rotten hypocrite without first having a will of one's own.

Americans have that freedom. For their own benefit or that of the group, perhaps even that of the whole nation, an individual enters into covenants of various stripes. The covenants describe the individual. A Southern Baptist, for example. A point guard in college basketball. A marathon runner, a bass fisherman, a sophomore at college. A member of the Saturday night bridge gang. A spouse. In the natural world, happiness may be something slowly won. In the human world, each covenant taken in advance brings comfort and happiness likewise in advance, from an arrangement warmly accepted.

Looking on the negative side of civilized circumstances, however, people who have a will of their own can be slimy, rotten hypocrites. Perhaps that is not news to you.

Individuals commonly have to decide what they absolutely swear they will do and what they promise with equal sincerity they will never do. Whatever activity it covers, that covenant beckons to hypocrisy. And then cheating.

The cheating to be dragged out of the shadows in this book covers a range of examples: from marital infidelity to business fraud, to school cribbing to sports deception. While some of the cheaters ended up in jail, laws are not the rules that underlie everyday cheating. The fear of getting arrested by the police is very different from the unthinkable cataclysm of getting *caught* by someone one knows personally. Tax cheating, for example, is not emphasized in the book as much as flower-show cheating. Both emanate from the same priority on self-interest. The finer point is that native-born Americans never specifically agree to abide by laws. Just as in the South before the Civil War, people in certain pockets of the backcountry today contend that they don't have to follow laws they don't like. This "nullification," as it was once called, gives zealots an out, at least where their sense of honor is concerned. They may be crooks, moonshiners, and tax holdouts—but they aren't cheats.

Neatly sidestepping a discussion of the individual in democracy (and whether representation itself conveys a covenant), I hold that breaking the law is not necessarily cheating.

Academic observers have expressed the opinion that everybody cheats. Lowlifes and barflies have made the same point. All men cheat. All women cheat. All lawyers cheat. All pitchers cheat. Everybody. That conclusion glistens with the cynicism that serves to protect academics as well as lowlifes. It so happens that I'm cynical, too. My credentials are irrefutable: I think the world stinks; I think we insult rats when we use their name to describe people; I am blissfully at home with early-1930s movies, the ones in which all the characters are corrupt. I know the score, as they used to say, circa 1933. Yet I'm unable to make the statement that everybody cheats, being that I'm tinged with the same sentimentality that causes many people to point to their parents as the two individuals on earth who absolutely, resolutely never could have cheated on each other or anyone else. If we can all agree that we each have a touchstone, knowledge of one or two people who are incapable of cheating, then we can make the calculation that there must be, empirically, some number of human beings who simply are not cheaters. That is the supposition of this book. And if you who are cynical don't bring me evidence that my selected paragons were cheating out loud every day and twice on Fridays, then I'll leave yours alone, too. It's an important point, because this study is as much about those who absolutely will not cheat as about those who can and then do.

Victims are also to be considered. If there are people who shirk rules that they once embraced, then there are necessarily those left behind, holding firm to the same covenant. The cheater and the cheated. The sole exception to the duality is cheating at solitaire—which is as baffling as it is surprisingly rampant. In solitaire, no one will be the wiser. Go ahead. Dig through for the last king. In every other instance, though, cheating leaves a gash in someone else's life. The popular pap that "cheaters only cheat themselves" is so untrue that it is cruel to repeat it—except in quotes, as though held out with tongs.

"Cheaters only cheat themselves," so satisfying as a phrase, leads to nowhere. The one covenant that is in no way implicit, the deal that individuals have with themselves, is an impression left by their sense of morality. Being so deeply personal, it occupies a wide plain, impossible to see or to map. For that reason, the great religions leave it to someone more qualified, someone ethereal, to judge whether a person has cheated him- or herself. If Mr. X's sole desire on this mortal span is to pile up money and he manages it by nefarious means, observers would be presumptuous in the extreme to suggest in a weak and yet hopeful voice that he had only cheated himself. In the flintier world of this study, we can't say if Mr. X cheated himself, but we can certainly accuse him of being blithely aware that he was going to rook others, even before he did so.

The corollary is less often heard, perhaps because everyone already knows it, probably from experience. It tends to remain in the system a long, long time. It's terribly un-catchy. The corollary: "Cheaters are fully aware in advance that they are going to stomp on some-one else and they do it anyway." That epithet is the second defining factor of cheating.

If cheaters don't all have the same basal values, nei-ther do people who are cheated. In a whole sector of betrayal, blaming the victim is absolutely the right thing to do, because a great many cheaters are drawn by an invisible force to their own kind. Outright hypocrisy and abject hurt: the cheating in this book covers the bright ideas behind a variety of adventures. Embracing people much smarter than I and those even dumber, the goal was to look at them all on eye level.

In this particular field, famous stars are not as in-teresting as humans who are drawn to scale, despite the fact that celebrity scandals are a mainstay of mod-ern life. A deluge, in fact. They don't count herein, though, because their lives are not merely exaggerated but also skewed. In certain celebrity circles, an extra-marital affair isn't an act of betrayal—it's a good career move. The stubborn shadow of a happy marriage, on the other hand, has to be overcome by a team of agents and a clever publicist. In the world of finance, even the U.S. Treasury Department can barely trace what multi-national companies are doing below-board. Or more specifically, what they are doing on those island nations with unending dunes and one office building. As to the intrinsic cheating found in super-rich families, it is far better described by America's great novelists; start with Fitzgerald and then consult Wharton, Dreiser, and James. In most sports, uniquely, cheating doesn't even exist—not until a player has been caught three times first.

In one bastion, politics, the ramifications were exactly the opposite of those in the celebrity world. Attitudes toward cheating were once super-normal—that is, the starchiest of standards applied to politicians, abruptly ending careers, except in rare cases when voters daintily forgave an indiscretion. That shifted in 2016, when voters who were confronted by a reflex of cheating on the part of Donald Trump admired it as a mark of strength. The new development came upon America so bluntly, it brought with it a revelation about just exactly who is the driving force behind America and cheating, an accord that has become a kinship of acceptance, embrace, and even dependence.

But don't blame Trump. He brought no particular innovation to cheating. Anyone might have filled his place as the first admitted cheater to be elected president, because that place had already been so thoroughly prepared by others: many millions—in fact, all of us, the passersby in American life. Whether we voted for him or not, we wanted cheating to be part of the national character. We must have.

SECTION ONE

You Who Are Cheated

CHAPTER 1

Your Own Kind

Why cheating is so hard to confront

In the movie *Scent of a Woman* (1992), a teenaged boy struggling for social acceptance at a prep school knows which of his fellow students dumped a bucket of paint on the headmaster's new Jaguar XJS coupe, a crime of vandalism. And an act of desecration in the eyes of automobile fans in the audience. Throw paint on the headmaster, throw it on the scrambled eggs at breakfast, throw it on each other, but not on a great-looking car. Viewers able to move past that point saw the plot build to a speech by the boy's erstwhile mentor, a cocksure Army veteran who exhorted him to never—ever, ever, ever—tattle on his friends. My personal loyalties in this matter may or may not be relevant, but I've been waiting since 1992 to make the rousing counter-assertion that when it comes to mistreatment of helpless Jaguar cars, I will tattle the bejesus out of my friends. Every time. Thank you.

In the broader world, denouncing a cheater can't be simplified as easily. The cards, as it were, are stacked against the person who has been wronged, as well as those nearby. By design, every stage of response is or seems to be fraught with risk, starting with the expressions used for the very act of calling out a cheater: snitching, squealing, blowing somebody in, ratting somebody out. And the names for that person: a weasel, a square, a stoolie, a toady, a stick-in-the-mud, a fink. On the list of neutral terms, there is "whistleblower." If, however, one wants to express admiration for a victim of cheating who pushes back, the words dry up. English, the richest of all human languages— its universe rippling with idioms—is at a loss. "Self righteous jerk" is the closest we have to an honorific for those who speak up.

While those who have been cheated try on the soubriquets, wondering whether "rat" or "double-crosser" has a better ring, the act of cheating awaits a reaction. In the majority of cases, it never comes. Among modern Americans trying to do the right thing, the desire for integrity leads to two avenues of diametrically opposite behavior. Turn in a cheater, you have character. Protect a cheater, you have *character*.

History pinpoints the time when Americans slipped into confusion—and comfort. It was when formalized social groups grew from almost nothing to dominate American life in the late 1800s—after the Civil War, not surprisingly, it being the ultimate disruption. Clubs became the rage. A new enthusiasm for hobbies brought people together, sports teams drew both players and fans to one side against all comers, while lodges solidified the values of the membership, and even colleges, which had once been educational institutions, nothing more, became cults in which alumni were even more invested than students. Circa 1835, T-shirt royalties didn't actually contribute much to the University of Alabama's budget. More recently, licensing of the school's name, mostly on apparel, brings in $13 million per year. That's not for shirts. Instead, the money gives millions of people a secure place smack in the middle of the Crimson Tide (unless the wearer shows up in Baton Rouge, Louisiana, or Clemson, South Carolina, in which case nothing will be secure, but that is part of the excitement). Within most colleges, fraternities rose to full flower in the same decades of the late 1800s, growing from lodging or dining houses into secret societies, where loyalty was the sole necessity, aside from the ability to withhold barf until the lawn was located. They were soon joined by sororities.

The abiding confidence across America was that social alliances would stabilize the country. That confidence long outlasted the post–Civil War days. It's now central to the image of a trustworthy American.

The philosophy that good members make good citizens trickled into school systems. Like colleges, they changed. Education was one mission and another was transforming the inclination to bond into a jam-packed twelve-hour schedule. Children are described not as who they are, but as who they are with.

"I happen to know for a fact that one of the boys in our class copied a book report word for word from a magazine," wrote a student in Longview, Texas. "That wouldn't make me so mad, except that he got an A+ for the assignment, and I only got a C+ for a paper I really worked on. I just happened to see the original browsing through the local library and compared it with the guy's report, which was on the lit [literary] room bulletin board. He didn't even change a comma! I don't know what to do."

In the very first place, if the literature teacher couldn't differentiate the work of a professional writer from that of a schoolboy, then either the teacher or the writer was cheating their employer.

More to the point, the Longview student, the one who received a C+, was already well-trained in peer loyalty. As people grow up in America, they're pressed constantly to ally themselves with others. Much of the school day is devoted to inculcating comradeship: in band and chorus, on sports teams (even individual sports are transformed into group efforts), in numerous clubs and theatrical shows, and in class projects designed to encourage cooperation. School pride encourages students to think of themselves as a part of a bigger group and so does class pride. The oddest aspect of the pressure to bond at a young age is that popularity in the world of public schools doesn't refer to the students who are well-liked. The popular kids are the ones who won't talk to anyone but each other. The normies are the ones who are liked, to some degree. The tough guys and the mean girls aren't liked at all, but they get their way. So on through a social scale that couldn't exist without willing adherents, first in homage to the social scale itself and, more important, to an underlying value system that is based in wholehearted acceptance of consensus—in all things.

A standout, except in sports, has a terrible problem. As a matter of fact, school is the only place where you certainly can be too rich or too thin.

While kids are sporadically told that cheating is wrong, they're continuously influenced to be loyal to their peers. The two directives are simultaneously at odds and coincident. Those who do cheat blow the bond sky-high—and yet they are protected by it. They will be addressed directly in the second section of this book. This section, the first, features the deeper conundrum, which lies with the cheated. They may be the ones smacked with trouble by the cheater, but they are also under pressure to keep mum and be predictable.

According to the testimony of the Longview student, the boy's blatant copying all by itself "wouldn't make me so mad." The generic reasons to resent plagiarism—it's lazy, it's stealing, it stinks out loud, and so on—had obviously failed to take hold. If the incident were to mean anything at all, the Longview student had to be damaged personally. Even then, with solid evidence in hand, the student paused. Whatever else happened after that, it was the student in the right who froze, as though caught in the act of being honest.

I remember a similar incident when, for extra credit, the sixth graders in our local school were invited to select an ancient Greek temple and build a wooden model of it. On the morning that the temples were displayed on a long table in the back of the classroom, the teacher proudly surveyed about a half-dozen striking replicas made out of hardwood and crafted in such exacting detail that the Greek government could have arrayed them at the embassy in Washington. Little models of ancient Greeks probably would have arrived soon after to worship. Next to those replicas and at the end of the line was a temple taped together out of balsa wood, Elmer's Glue-All oozing out of the crevices. Its builder had bypassed masterpieces of architecture honoring Apollo and Athena—with colonnades, pediments, and grand steps, straight and true—finding instead a picture of an ancient Greek temple shaped like a car wash. Even so, in miniature at the back of the classroom, it leaned. Once the display was up, dads were on hand to take photos and carefully nudge the other temples to the perfect center of their painted bases. The builder of the last temple didn't dare touch it. Or breathe on it. Quite obviously, that intrepid little person was up against the *fathers* of the other students, grown men who had woodworking shops in their basements.

I...was that sloppy little person. Like the Longview student, I received a grade of C (C– to be specific) and never once piped up about the cheating displayed along the rest of the table—not because I was cowed by the other students, but because I was afraid of accusing their fathers.

The Longview student, whose letter to an advice column succinctly repeats the predicament of many others, signed the name "Furious" and yet stalled out when it came to action. Something was more important than fairness; something was more important than grades. Why wouldn't that student pipe up, being on the side of right? As one of many others in the same category, I will interrogate myself on that question:

Q: Why didn't you say something about the other temples having been built by ringers?

A: I knew some of the fathers personally. After all, they were just trying to help.

Q: Who made you into Athena, goddess of justice? The fact is, their kids cheated. *They* cheated.

A: Well, I knew I was a terrible woodworker.

Q: Getting back to the point: they cheated.

A: I wasn't afraid of *losing* in an argument with the fathers, had I gone ahead and accused them of cheating. I was afraid of winning.

Q: Your Honor, permission to treat as a hostile witness—

A: The other kids already thought I was bossy. I couldn't court-martial the fathers... I'd never live it down.

Q: The bond. Here we have it. Conformity in our society is not only the mark of the bond, it's what makes cheaters sleep well at night.

A: This is my book. Could I have it back, please?

So anyway, conformity in our society is not only the mark of the bond, it's what makes cheaters sleep well at night.

In the case of the Longview student, the columnist answering the letter duly upheld what is widely referred to as the students' code: "Thou shalt not fink."

Specifically, she substituted "Thou shalt not be caught finking," which passes for an honorable alternative. The columnist's advice to the Longview student was this: wait until the classroom is empty and then leave the magazine on the teacher's desk, opened to the plagiarized book review. The teacher would be bound to notice it there.

In the first place, every teacher in America comes into the classroom with an armful of papers, books, brochures for distant cruises, and a cup of coffee. All of that would be set down immediately on top of that least noticeable of all items: a magazine open to a book review.

For more significant, if less practical reasons, though, the columnist's advice is still remarkable. It flutters straight past integrity, without even a nod in that direction. The kid who was in the right is supposed to stoop to the level of a sneak in order to preserve a bond with the plagiarizer. That's what is most important. In one stroke, the columnist deftly proved that the opposite of self-respect isn't dishonesty; it's expediency. In order to get the job done and unmask a cheater without collateral damage, you're forced to become a trespasser in your own world. Far more satisfying would be a picture of the Longview student waiting until class was about to begin, the kids, including the cheater, in their seats, and then— as everyone watched in perfect silence—strutting up to the lit room bulletin board to pin the magazine article right next to the plagiarized book report. That would make for a better story, but not necessarily for a better result in the real world.

Authorities have their own reasons for protecting the status quo. The teacher might easily see the magazine clipping as it was being pinned to the board, sidle up to it, and read the verbatim evidence of copying. And still choose to use the review as a coaster for the coffee cup.

The Philadelphia Phillies catcher Andy Seminick became an expert on all the ways a pitcher could doctor a baseball before throwing it. He'd seen every kind of glop attached to the ball. Under the umbrella term "spitball," the idea is that any foreign substance or damage to the ball makes it take an unexpected path to the plate, fooling the batter. In one game, Seminick was playing against the right-handed pitcher Gaylord Perry. Each time he took the field, he was handed the ball that Perry had just been using. "I saw one of his," Seminick reported, "that had a big spot of Vaseline on it." He had the big rightie dead-to-rights. "I showed it to the umpire," Seminick continued. "He said, 'What are you going to do about it?' and wiped it off."

Baltimore Orioles pitcher Jim Palmer went out to the mound during a matchup with Perry, looked down at the game ball, and saw a thumbprint in some oily substance, if not Vaseline, then perhaps baby oil. Palmer didn't present the ball to the umpires as proof of cheating on the other side. He picked it up and played the game. Such examples were commonly traded in baseball chatter, and if they were lacking, Perry was happy to supply them. Over the course of decades, opposing players learned that there was no choice except to shrug off Perry's shenanigans and play ball. The presumption, in fact, was that Perry gained even more out of his reputation as a cheat than from any actual cheating. If batters were watching for a loaded ball, they were distracted: advantage Perry.

Twenty-one years into Perry's career, he was finally tossed from a game for throwing an illegal ball. Twenty-one years, in the middle of which he published a book about throwing the "spitter." One of the many beauties of baseball is that it has a sense of humor and actually smirks at a colorful player like Perry titling his 1974 book *Me and the Spitter*. At the height of his career, he explained how he could manage to doctor the ball standing on a mound observed by thousands of people in the stands and, more important, by one opposing manager, grinding his teeth in the dugout. He even compiled a long list of liquids, including everything short of molten lava, that he said he brought out to the field hidden on his person. The book was published and enjoyed a wide readership—and then Perry played nine more seasons. That is not to say that baseball is the only field in which a self-advertised cheater will be treated with front-porch hospitality. But Perry, trailing accusations like so many kids seeking autographs, swept into the Baseball Hall of Fame in 1990. The question is no longer what he was doing. It's what the umps were doing, when they didn't care what he was doing.

In the world of backroom poker, on the other hand, no authority exists. That's probably part of the appeal of a floating game in such a well-ordered, constantly chaperoned society: in case of complaint, there is no number to dial. You are your own big brother. The rules are well known to everyone at the table and that's all there is of government in the generic sense. Into such a game stepped the dumbest cheater—of all time.

Louis DiGiulio was a wiseguy in Rochester, New York, with a reputation as a minor member of the Mafia in town. About twenty-five years old, he was playing poker late one night with a circle of tough characters—decidedly not a friendly game. If there is such a thing as a friendly game. The realm of dirty poker is vast, separating into three primary specialties; the first two are crooked dealing and peeking at opponents' cards. DiGiulio chose the third major technique, the one with the highest degree of difficulty: exchanging cards.

Not only did DiGiulio have to prepare ahead of time, gingerly placing cards up his sleeve, but he had to be practiced at maneuvering them as needed—absconding, for example, with the six of clubs he'd been dealt and dropping an ace into his hand instead. At the opportune point in the late-night game with the boys from Rochester, when only he and one other player were still in the hand, he made a switch. All eyes were on him as he responded to the other man's call by fanning his cards on the table—the winning hand. They hadn't noticed that he'd swapped cards. No sensation is better than that of making a hoe of one's hands and hauling in a mass of chips, unless it is that same feeling accompanied by the intoxication of relief. Money is good, but getting away with something is better. While DiGiulio casually pulled in the chips from the center of the table, the other players grumbled and the next dealer gathered the cards, turning them facedown and stacking them up in a way that put the hand safely into history. Flipping DiGiulio's cards over, the dealer suddenly balked. A split second later, the other players looked down and saw what he was staring at. Four red-backed cards and one blue-backed one.

The man who had lost the hand didn't know what to do, under the circumstances. DiGiulio, in his own account later on, admitted that "he'd caught me red-handed." And partly blue-handed, of course, but the point is that in yet another circumstance, the evidence of cheating was plain and it was the person cheated who didn't know what to do. Hard as it may be to believe, he didn't want to confront a strapping young mafioso hothead. Yet, he couldn't let it rest, either. He was in the blurry part of the present tense reserved for those who have just been cheated.

"I apologized to the guy for cheating," DiGiulio said later, "but he wouldn't stop griping and complaining." When DiGiulio had had enough, he suddenly turned grim and walloped the complainer. As the man crumpled to the floor, DiGiulio ran out the door.

A few years later, a defense attorney forced DiGiulio to relate that story when he appeared in court as the star prosecution witness in a murder trial concerning a hit on a prominent union official in Rochester. "You're a cheater at cards, aren't you?" the lawyer asked.

"Yeah, a bad one," DiGiulio said with a grin. A murder trial is no place for high spirits, but the courtroom burst into laughter. As DiGiulio continued to testify about his dirty poker, people in the courtroom were smiling, chuckling, and breaking out in claps of laughter. The defense attorney had miscalculated. If DiGiulio got away with cheating the man in the back room, then he had got away with it for good. The people in the courtroom, part of the great overlap of those who love a winner and those who overlook a cheater, were pulled to his side, amid the merriment. Laughter is the very best of human traits; at the base, it's also an exhibition of accord, both with the merry-maker and other laughers. When the proper response to tales of Perry's spitballs grew to be a cackle, the bond became all but unbreakable. Likewise, when the jury broke with court etiquette and giggled at DiGiulio's exploits at the poker table, the bond of laughter rendered the cheater immune.

As to the man who had been bilked that night in the back room, he eventually stood up from the floor and went home, bruised and quite alone, and still grumbling quietly to himself. That is the universal portrait of a person who has just been cheated.

CHAPTER 2

To Be or Not to Cheat

People who never cheat

On November 15, 1955, a woman in her twenties made national news by appearing on a quiz show in a New York studio to answer a question written especially for her: "What are the ring names of the four heavyweight boxing champions whose real names are Rocco Marchegiano, Arnold Raymond Cream, Joseph Paul Zukauskas, and Noah Brusso?"

The difficulty of that question may come as a shock, especially to anyone who has had the enlightening experience of watching British quiz shows recently. A person never feels more truly American than when sitting stone-faced and silent through a British quiz show. On a counterpart American show, the contestant gets a new truck for knowing whether Brazil is in Australia...*or not*. On British shows, the contestant lists the Brazilian presidents in order, includes their spouses, names their mistresses or gigolos, also in order, and wins a five-pound note. Things were different in the mid-1950s, however. In that era, quiz shows in America asked questions that were impossible for many contestants to answer. Some of them answered anyway.

As necessary, contestants received the answers in advance. It didn't have to be heavy-handed, though. Apparently, in many cases, players didn't even know they were getting the answers; at lunch with one of the producers, the conversation would amiably meander into some arcane topic, as it often does at lunch. "Have another dessert, sure, you bet, it's on the network tab...I was just sitting here thinking about Getúilio Vargas—there was a man, don't you think?...Haven't you? During World War II, he was president of Brazil, but—No. Nope. Actually, it's in South America...Anyway, Getúilio Vargas was there during World War II, with U-boats and spies and all that, but what's really interesting, if you ask me, is that his wife's name was Darci."

Backstage small talk might subsequently lead a lighting man or a receptionist to mention the latest rumor going around, that Aimée Lopez de Sottomaior was Getúilio Vargas's mistress before World War II! Most of the contestants who received their answers before the show chalked it up to showbiz. Only one regarded it as cheating. An impoverished poet from Greenwich Village was on *The $64,000 Question* when he realized that the idle remarks made to him by the producers during the day just happened to be the answers to the questions he was being asked as the show progressed. The drama onscreen was real, as the poet squirmed in his seat, tortured by the realization that he was cheating.

He looked as though he were about to stalk off the set, but instead, he quietly murmured the answers to the questions. As the show ended, he was at $4,000 and being invited back to continue the following week. That's when he stalked out. No one at the network ever saw him again and the money that he had earned, if not won, went uncollected.

The $64,000 Question purposefully lined up people and their categories against "type"—the policeman whose area of expertise was Shakespeare, the jockey whose area was fine art. The recent immigrant whose category was American history. Among other reasons for that, most people who purport some level of knowledge professionally were loath to risk embarrassment on national television.

Due to the anomalous character of most of the contestants, viewers commonly wondered if they were indeed being fed answers. It wasn't a sharp cause for concern, just a means of explaining how all the wrong people had all the right answers. At first glance, the underhanded ways of *The $64,000 Question* wouldn't even fall into the definition of cheating. Was Fay Wray cheating when she screamed while being carried up the Empire State Building by a giant ape? There was no ape, after all. *King Kong* wasn't real, just entertainment. The game show producers argued that entertainment was their only business, too.

The government disagreed. On two levels, the programs were subjected to high-level investigations—just exactly as though TV quiz shows mattered. The district attorney of New York County, Frank S. Hogan, a tough bird who served for over thirty years, convened the grand jury to delve into charges of cheating at quiz shows. As remarkable, the U.S. House of Representatives investigated the same charge, with sharp staffers actually basing their whole careers on whether some lowly government warehouse clerk actually knew the name of the canals used in Union flanking expeditions at the Battle of Vicksburg. One might think that the whole matter could have been handled by an even more lowly clerk at the Federal Communications Commission, calling the producers into a gray building in Washington and reading the bylaws of good broadcasting out loud to them. In the later 1950s, however, the quiz shows had added interest to the government. First, as the purported missile gap and the actual space race gained the fearful attention of America, the quality of education at all levels elicited impassioned debate. America's intellectual superiority became a priority of national concern. Second, television was growing more powerful than any other medium and no end was in sight for its influence over the population—once the purview of politicians. The chance to display supremacy over television in a highly public way came along at the right time for elected officials.

The investigators from the government found that the producers of The $64,000 Question were manipulative on many levels. When a contestant was fun, magnetic, or simply entertaining, the questions eased up a bit, or leaned toward the player's specific expertise—not merely geology, for example, but volcanic geology. Likewise, when the producers wanted to end a contestant's run on the show, they would pick out a far tougher question, flipping through possibilities written out on index cards, sometimes even while watching from the control room. If a contestant had worn out their welcome, the producer had an absurdly difficult question ready to ensure their exit.

On November 15, 1955, it was time for the boxing expert to get bounced. But she had other ideas. Dr. Joyce Brothers was later famous in her own right as a psychologist, but in 1955, she was just another face in the Manhattan crowd. Married to a physician and mother of an infant girl, she had graduated from Cornell University before taking advanced degrees from Columbia in psychology. When she applied to go on the quiz show, she suggested that she could answer questions on homemaking or psychology. The producers looked at her—a homemaker and psychologist— and rejected those ideas. As an aside, one producer said she'd have a better chance of getting on the show if she were an expert on wrestling or boxing. He was just trying to make a point, but Dr. Brothers spent the next month and a half memorizing facts about boxing. She then duly appeared on the show, making her way through the early rounds, week by week. On November 15, she barely had to think about her question, regarding the ring names of Rocco Marchegiano, Arnold Raymond Cream, Joseph Paul Zukauskas, and Noah Brusso.

"Rocky Marciano, Jersey Joe Walcott, Jack Sharkey, and Tommy Burns," she answered.

The producers were less than pleased. Far from slipping her the answers in future episodes, they brought in bona fide experts to help concoct questions that were as close to impossible as could be. The suspense across the country was nothing compared to that in the control room. Each week, Dr. Brothers sat in the "isolation booth," waiting for her question. Each week, she dispensed correct answers. On December 6, 1955, with the grand prize of $64,000 at stake, she answered a six-part question, ranging from "What was the name of the glove worn by Roman gladiators?" (*cestus*) to "How long did the Dempsey–Firpo match last?" (three minutes, fifty-seven seconds). Just as Dr. Brothers supplied the last answer, production staffers with headsets heard the response from the control room: "Oh, shit."

When asked boxing questions after her reign, Dr. Brothers typically refused, protesting that her mind was like a sink; once she was through with a collection of information, she opened the drain and forgot it all. That description of her memory may have held some truth, but she was nothing if not ambitious and she wanted to be a television or radio psychologist (a profession not even extant in 1955); to that end, what she really wanted to jettison down a drain was her reputation as a boxing genius. Nonetheless, in 1958, Dr. Brothers was called before District Attorney Hogan's grand jury. A number of other former *$64,000 Question* players had already admitted to some level of cheating, but she insisted that she'd been upright.

According to Dr. Brothers's later account, the grand jury proceedings on the day she appeared became the most suspenseful quiz show of them all, and also the longest. The prize had nothing to do with money. Dr. Brothers's reputation was on trial. Since the prosecutors didn't have proof that she had cheated, they decided to establish that she couldn't have succeeded in any other way. In order to prove the negative, so elusive in courtrooms everywhere, the attorneys, along with members of the jury, peppered her with boxing questions. For six hours, she batted answers right back. "The grand jury asked me boxing questions all day long and I got every one right," Dr. Brothers said twenty-three years later. "I came out a hero." She proved that she hadn't cheated by showing that she didn't have to.

In a setting preoccupied with applying showbiz shortcuts to a real situation, Dr. Brothers had not been tempted.

Five considerations underscore the decision not to cheat. The primary one for the vast majority of people is the chance of getting caught. If the possibility seems nonexistent, then cheating has been proven clinically to be irresistible to a large part of the population. Casinos installed ceiling cameras in a sudden wave in the 1960s—more so to dissuade potential cheats than to catch active ones. The second factor in the decision on cheating is the desirability of what can be gained. The third is the desirability of whatever might be lost. The fourth consideration is the degree to which someone else may be harmed—and that isn't always a negative in the equation. Sometimes, it is a plus. The final factor of the five is the balance of effort against the other four factors.

Everyone who thinks about cheating, however fleetingly, has their own abstraction of the relative values of the five. Expressing the factors as an equation, however, allows a law of math to cross over into that very human calculation, because if any of the factors is judged to be nil, zed, or not-in-a-million-years, then the decision to cheat is almost automatically not-in-a-million-years. Just as one can stop listening early on when quizzed on the total of zero times eight times four times and so on—it's going to be zero if there's a zero in the column—the decision for people who do not cheat can rest on a single factor, whether they think further or not.

> **Rate the following.** Any zero means no cheating.
> Decision to Cheat:
> ____ 0 to 10: *Chance of GETTING AWAY with It*
> x ____ 0 to 10: *Value of What Can Be GAINED*
> x ____ 0 to 10: *Ability to Live without Whatever Can Be LOST*
> x ____ 0 to 10: *Certainty that No One Else Can Be HARMED*[*][†]
> **divided by:**
> ____ 1 to 100: *Aversion to the BOTHER Involved*
> **KEY:** Scores of 50 or above predict that you will cheat.

Inasmuch as the equation reflects the thinking of a fraction of a second, a national audience watched as the impoverished poet on the quiz show thought his decision through. He had every reason to cheat—except one. First, he was already in the midst of getting away with it. He had $4,000 to be gained; no one else would be harmed—except the entire American

---

[*] If the cheating is specifically designed as punishment (see chapter 3), invert this factor to *Certainty that Someone Else Will Be Harmed.*

[†] Because "who cares" as an answer is not a number, delete this line entirely if you are the only person on the planet who matters.

viewing audience—and the work was already done. But he didn't want to lose whatever he had arrived with. That included the right to call the rest of the world bitter names, in rhyming couplets, if he preferred. Furthermore, he had walked in with his integrity, which he took back with him to Greenwich Village.

In the case of Dr. Brothers, absolutely nothing desirable could be gained by cheating. She was already a repository for boxing trivia, a walking encyclopedia in every sense except the anatomical. It sometimes happens that those who don't cheat just don't have to. Financially, emotionally, athletically, or in any other way, including boxing trivially, no gaps wait to be filled. One husband had a pragmatic reason for why he had no interest in committing adultery: "My wife knows how to press my buttons sexually and I know exactly what she likes. Where could I find another woman who could do me right?" Not exactly a Rodgers & Hammerstein lyric, but it has a certain lilt.

It would fit three-quarter time.

To another group, the desirability of what can be gained is also represented by "zero." Because its occupants are virtuous doesn't mean they are saintly. It is the category of supreme egomaniacs and pigheads. Also, snotheads. That is said with the utmost respect. They are people with the attitude that *if it isn't mine, I don't want it* (where "it" can also be a man or a woman), along with the corollary, *if it isn't mine, it is a piece of trash* (where "trash" can also refer to a man or woman). Vanity precludes such people from stooping to admit that they are lacking in any way. The key to their refusal to cheat is that others should envy them, their lives, their assignations and their possessions—not vice versa.

The measurement of the chance of getting caught was never easier than at the luxurious Eden Roc Hotel in Miami Beach, where a Jewish banker had paid for a wedding for his daughter and her intended, specifying that the reception for 365 guests afterward was to be kosher. The ingredients had to be procured from specialized butchers and other suppliers, before being prepared in a certain way and under strict rabbinical supervision. When the banker added sixty guests at the last minute, however, the chef had no choice but to sneak some non-kosher steaks into the kitchen. It was too late to get kosher ones.

Cooks at work preparing a gourmet dinner for 425 people are known to be tense—a badly tied bundle of dangerous emotions. Into that kitchen at that moment strode the city's kosher inspector, Frank Brickman. He homed in on the steaks. (One suspects there had been a tip-off.) Oblivious to the 425 hungry guests on the other side of the wall, he wanted to see the meat tags for each individual steak, along with the receipt from a kosher butcher. The Eden Roc called the banker into the kitchen. Everyone looked at the 425 thick red steaks awaiting the grill. Tender they may have looked, inviting they may have been, but some of them were non-kosher. No one knew which.

The dilemma in the heat of that kitchen is reminiscent of the one in Moscow in the 1860s, when the vogue in court circles was for a delicate yellow cake invented by one of the royal bakers. It gained legions of fans during teatime, a paramount event in old Moscow.

Two of the main ingredients were eggs and milk, however, both of which were forbidden during Lent in the Russian Orthodox Church. Without the cakes, teatime seemed like a bore. Guests at court were literally glum until news spread that the baker had concocted a substitute cake recipe for the Lenten season, one that didn't require either eggs or milk. Once again, princes and countesses, grand duchesses and counts gobbled them up, redoubling their praise for the ingenious baker. They weren't particularly interested in cooking or curious how he did it, but a visiting Englishman who spoke Russian couldn't resist the mystery and searched him out. The baker was bustling around the ovens when he was asked how he could make the cakes without butter and eggs.

"You want to know how I make them taste the same?" he replied.

"Yes, I'm damned curious."

"I use butter and eggs."

The banker in Miami returned to the banquet room and called for attention. He wasn't going to lie. The chef could've lied, if Brickman hadn't been standing in the kitchen, but the banker had no choice. He waited for silence and at least eight hundred hungry eyes turned to him. He explained that the steaks had been mixed up and the cooks couldn't tell which were kosher and which were not. Anyone wishing to have an uncertifiable steak could still have one. Anyone keeping kosher, however, would have to skip the steak.

A certain equation flickered through the room. As Brickman recalled it, "Even the Jews who would have eaten non-kosher didn't want to stand up and say so."

The result was inevitable; the wedding reception became a vegetarian event.

Inasmuch as eating non-kosher food was a type of cheating for strict adherents to Jewish law, the odds of getting caught at the Eden Roc that day were inescapably high. "So nobody ate meat that night," Brickman said, with the satisfaction of a man who had saved untold numbers of people from themselves.

The late Sheela Allen, an extremely bright television reporter in Philadelphia who was lovingly described by a colleague as "a walking event," was a student at a parochial school on Long Island when she built up a business in her classes with no fear of getting caught. And a business it was, as she charged seventy-five other students for the right answers on tests. Remarkably, she had specific codes for each student, all transmitted by her nose: sniffles, sneezes, use of a handkerchief, and so on, such that only paying customers could decode her data. The girl turned her nostrils into the Enigma machine. She even supplied the answers for essay tests. "I had seventy-five signals for seventy-five people," she said. "Sister Grace Anne used to think I had a sinus problem.

"But Sister Mary," Sheela continued, "caught me giving answers and threw me out of school."

Personally, I would have let Sheela run the school.

"Sister Mary and my mother prayed together for my soul," Sheela continued. "They gave me a St. Jude's medallion—the patron of hopeless cases." She wore the medallion around her neck for years and then kept it in her pocketbook all the time. She was a brilliant cheater with a tremendous future in the field, but the experience at school left her with a permanent "zero" for "Ability to live without whatever can be lost." For all others, her story stands as a reminder that anybody can get caught, even the smartest person in sight.

In the working-class town of Pennsauken, New Jersey, four-year-old Ron Brook frequently walked with his mother down 35th Street to the corner of Federal Street, the main drag, to buy a few items at Kessel's delicatessen. For a big food order, his father drove the family to a supermarket ten blocks away, but Kessel's was walking distance. Even though the family didn't have much money to spare, his father would splurge on Chuckles candy at the supermarket and split the box with his son. Mrs. Brook didn't spend money on candy. She grew up with even tighter finances, her parents having arrived in Pennsylvania from southern Italy with little except immense pride at having made it to America. One day, Ron wandered out of his mother's view at Kessel's. When the two of them arrived back home, he showed her a piece of bubble gum. The price was a penny, but he hadn't had to pay. He took it!

My own family wryly taught me never to steal less than a life-changing amount of money: a billion, a hundred million, a trillion. For Ron, the penny was life-changing. "My mother immediately walked me back to the store to return the gum to the owner," he said. "Mr. Kessel didn't smile; he didn't say, 'That's okay, sonny.' I felt like dirt."

The "wrath of my mother," as Ron termed it, kept him from entertaining further thoughts of getting something for nothing, in any sense. The factor that has kept him from it during a full life and a career as a reliability engineer was the far quieter realization that settled over him, standing all alone in front of Mr. Kessel. "My mother came from a poor Italian family from Altoona, Pennsylvania, and they were very conscientious about doing everything right: the law, manners, ethics, et cetera. At Kessel's, I felt so badly about what I had done and how it reflected on my family," he said, "that I never cheated anybody again or even entertained the thought." Hurting Mr. Kessel's bottom line by the amount of one cent was wrong, there is no denying. The possibility of harming one's own family, though, even to the extent of one cent is a starker deterrent to a great many in the ranks of the noncheaters.

Religious teachings also keep some adherents from the loose living of a cheat. Unfortunately, the word "cheating" wasn't known when most such wisdom was written down around the world. In the Bible, for example, ten thousand Commandments wouldn't begin to cover the many specific schemes covered by the word. "Thou shalt not point-shave (after basketball is invented)" didn't make the list and "Whatever you do, don't so much as glance at the babysitter" was apparently too wordy. A Biblical scholar once looked long and hard to find an exhortation against cheating in schoolwork and couldn't find a reference that applied directly. The Commandments do prohibit stealing, adultery, and coveting, three sins that attach to many forms of cheating, literally or in spirit.

The only trouble with wisdom is that it is subject to interpretation (which may explain why there have been over ten thousand religious sects in the history of

humanity). One religious writer in Missouri, for example, vehemently made the case that retired people who
spent money on themselves "cheated" their children by
"breaking God's commandment against stealing." Parents should deny themselves in old age, he insisted, so
that the kids would inherit more money. He no doubt
had an interesting home life, what with his mother and
father running from the room whenever he poured the
drinks. The religious basis for refusing to cheat is real,
however. The certain knowledge that eternal damna-
tion will follow sooner or later is a sense of loss and
it doesn't fade. If it did, we would have little in the
way of Spanish literature. Potential cheaters who look
to the aftermath don't necessarily mean the next couple
of weeks when they shudder once and then keep walking, avoiding the risk.

As to people for whom cheating is too much work
and bother, they are right. When George Burns
quipped in his nineties that "At my age, when a girl
turns me down, I thank her," he may have been speaking for many people of all ages, in terms of opportuni-
ties to cheat. It can be far more demanding than real
life, as in the prohibitive tale of the student who at-
tracted no particular attention during a crucial biology
test, looking intently through his microscope and then
jotting down his findings on the exam. Well in advance,
he had arduously and microscopically written all of the
information he needed for the test on a card the size of
a specimen slide. A born cheater apparently has a different view of hard work.

Not all graffiti is compelling. Not every human touch
is art. Not every rusty car is sculpture. But minute

writing that fits a whole course on a card the size of a stick of gum, that's an expression of the person inside the artifice. He was dumb—an appallingly bad biologist—but he had a point of view and that's something. For nearly anybody else, though, biology is easier than all that tiny writing.

People who will not cheat rarely have to think it over. Thinking, in fact, is a bad omen. Water will always find a way to do what it wants, slowly but eventually, and so will people who are giving careful consideration to cheating. The more usual path to a decision among habitual non-cheaters is bluntly drawn: zero to be gained, much to be lost, or in the case of that bravest of beings, the penniless snob: if I don't have it, thank you, no, I don't want it.

CHAPTER 3

Power Play

Cheating as punishment or

symbol of superiority

Way down in the bottom—whah the cotton boll's a rotten
Won't get my hundud all day.
Befo'e I'll be beated—befo'e I'll be cheated
I'll leave five finguhs in the boll
Befo'e I'll be beated—befo'e I'll be cheated
I'll leave five finguhs in the boll.
Black man beat me—white man cheat me
Won' get my hundud all day
Black man beat me—white man cheat me
Won' get my hundud all day.
—Song of African American cotton pickers in Georgia[*]

---

[*]   The job of the picker was to gather the cotton to the last wisp.
In the soggy bottomland, however, rot weakened the sectionalized
clump known as the five fingers at the low end of the boll. Prying
it out took extra time. The pickers were then caught between the
driver and the owner of the plantation. The driver (typically a
black man, as noted in the song) demanded each picker deliver
upward of a hundred pounds of cotton per day, but the owner, described as a white man, wouldn't accord credit for the full load
anyway.

Yellow Kid Weil, the legendary grifter who inspired the character of Henry Gondorff in *The Sting*, insisted that he conducted his business with the scruples of a bishop. He said that he "never took a dollar from a man who didn't deserve to lose it" due to his own avarice. In the parlance of the Chicago streets where he learned his ethics, the people he victimized were asking for it. The Yellow Kid was and still is admired as an ingenious cheater, one who added props, sets, and dramatic license to elegant schemes that took in millions of dollars. New York financiers made his life exciting, but it was small-town misers in the Midwest who provided him with a steady income.

At the height of his fame, the Yellow Kid asked an acquaintance for a donation to the Little Sisters of the Poor in Chicago. He was immediately given a check—of course. Who wouldn't want to support women devoted to caring for the elderly poor of all creeds and colors? The Yellow Kid took the check and then kept the money—three dollars. Possibly, he felt that the Sisters *deserved to lose* the three dollars. Possibly, he pocketed the money as a public service, to defuse the greedy ways of those big pirates, the Little Sisters. Or possibly, he saw no difference at all between bilking a Wall Street syndicate and shaving a gaggle of selfless Catholic women.

The Yellow Kid had one thing in common with the Little Sisters: He didn't differentiate religions. During a short stint in the penitentiary, he solicited funds from wealthy, Jewish Chicagoans, so that prisoners of the same faith could celebrate Passover. He kept that money, too. The Yellow Kid, for all of his gorgeous talk, only cared about the profit at the end of the cheat. And there is something to be admired in that and in all unmitigated selfishness. It has a humane purity about it, a crystalline logic unclouded by passion or bias. The alternative is the type of cheating that is weaponized to take aim at a particular person or type of person. It is an action of prejudice, intended to cheat the spirit, as well as the prospects, of the mark. That sort of cheater thrives a little in his heart only when the mark withers a lot in his.

"You have to be blind to realize how mean people can be," asserted Placido Santora, who lost his sight as an adult. Looking for a way to continue supporting his wife and two children, he decided to operate a newsstand.

"The other day," Santora said, "a man who seemed by his voice to be well-educated stopped and talked to me for a half hour. His sympathy cheered me so much. Finally, he took four magazines." The customer handed over paper money and Santora gave him the proper coins in change. After he left, Santora's wife came into the stand and found that the stranger had paid with fake money: worthless pieces of paper. "I broke down," Santora said, "and cried like a baby."

Not all cheaters consider what is to be gained as the prime motivation. For a large proportion of them, the person or entity to be cheated is even more important. The motivation itself can turn to a habit: correcting the standing order of one's world by making sure that someone else, someone in particular, is made smaller. In the case of the newsstand in New York, if the "man who seemed by his voice to be well-educated" walked away from the newsstand with a bounce in his step, it may not have anything to do with reading the magazines. It's perfectly possible that he threw them away on the next block.

In terms of the goods to be gained, that story could have occurred this morning, but in fact, it took place in 1921. At the time, the blind were in the midst of a long transition that belongs with others in the march of civil rights. For a long time in America, the blind in the lower classes were either pitied or else resented as parasites and de facto beggars. "Sighted people seem to think that all the blind are panhandlers," said the head of a charity devoted to reversing that attitude. "They can't seem to realize that a blind man has as much pride and self-respect as any sighted person. They will fling money at a blind beggar sooner than patronize a blind news dealer. But, although they give it to the beggar, they have an idea that he is putting one over on them, that he probably has a snug bank account. At that, they may be half right, for panhandling has remained the more lucrative profession."

"Do people try to cheat us? Do they honey!" laughed Fannie Lyons, who ran a newsstand with her husband. Both had long since lost their sight. "Stealing from the blind is one of the most popular outdoor sports in New York City," Mrs. Lyons declared. "I know a few tricks to protect myself, but it keeps me pretty busy to stay a lap ahead."

In the minds of people who felt actively compelled to put blind people at a lower level of status, two courses accomplished the same thing. Giving money to a beggar established superiority. Cheating for goods proclaimed it. Either of those acts aggrandized the sighted person possessed of a certain attitude—and according to Mrs. Lyons, there were plenty of them. The notion that was going out of style very slowly in 1921 was that the blind were to be pitied or despised, either of which tipped the beam in the same direction.

"I used to keep a little sign out," Santora said, "but I hide it now. It does no good." He rooted around under a stack of newspapers and felt for a placard. "Don't pity the blind," it read. "Help them to succeed." That pinpointed precisely what a segment of the population did not want to do.

The self-proclaimed right to either pity 'em or cheat 'em writes most of the ethnic history of the United States. Naturally, anyone newly arrived to the ways of European American culture can't be well-versed in its rules, a fact that makes them irresistible to people with ideas, people otherwise known as cheaters. Every immigrant American I've ever known, notably my relatives, loved America, willingly served in the armed forces or supported those who did, paid taxes as a patriotic act—and for as long as they lived, recoiled at the words "I've got a terrific deal for you" spoken in an American accent.

Some of those newly arrived groups never exactly volunteered to become part of the national culture. They included Indians, Hispanics in the Southwest, and African Americans. The compulsion to cheat Indians is well-documented, especially in nineteenth-century history, yet as an American syndrome, it has two unique features. The first has become a reflex over the past one hundred years: each and every generation in the mainstream firmly believes that it was only previous Americans who rooked Indians. The second is that careful studies of Indian nations have been conducted by European Americans almost since the birth of the United States, reflecting obvious fascination. Love, respect, and even idolatry, for Indian culture in combination with disrespect for Indian individuals is a balance that obviously feels right to European America, although as an undiluted European American, I can't quite see how.

When my newly arrived Irish ancestors were being shortchanged on a daily basis in New Jersey, nobody had romantic ideas about Irish people, with books of lore all over the house. Longfellow didn't write any poems about us. Buffalo Bill didn't bring us on tour, drawing bedazzled crowds to see real live Irish immigrants circle arenas in crowded streetcars. Frederic Remington didn't sell millions of four-color prints suitable for framing of my ancestor, depicting him as a chisel-faced American Irishman pausing on a promontory, surrounded by his family (in a used Cadillac), shielding his eyes from the sunset (with horn-rim Ray-Bans), his wife keeping the babies close ("Stop fightin' back there") as they broke a trail (on the Garden State) to find a new frontier (somebody said exit 40). On the contrary, the part of American history that makes sense—mostly because we now know it was temporary—is that nobody could stand the sight of my Irish forebears and concomitantly, people cheated them, left and right.

Okay.

The man who helped launch the serious apprecia-
tion of Indian cultures in the 1800s was Thomas Jefferson, unquestionably an American ideal. Certainly, he is
one of my ideals, admiring as I do his cerebral quality
and logical mind, his erudition, equanimity, and calm
demeanor. Perhaps it's an easy metaphor, but like the
country he helped found, he was far from perfect—yet
at least he tried, day in and day out, to improve. Less
metaphorically, if I ever meet him, I am going to punch
him out.

I've never had to say that about Pedro Martínez.

Eleanor Roosevelt or Franklin, either. Fred Astaire—
never.

Few Americans in the first days of the republic were
as intrigued as Jefferson with Indian cultures and languages. Nonetheless, as president, he consistently
cheated Indian nations that were in his way. In a letter
of 1803, he blithely explained to a newly appointed Indian agent in Tennessee how to fool the local Indian
chiefs into running up towering debts at the federal
stores so that they could then be forced into doing
whatever the government wanted—notably, into vacat-
ing their lands and moving with their tribes somewhere
to the west. The fact that Indians typically didn't understand American-style banking and debt was well-
known to Jefferson. It was part of his plan, which he
reiterated in other correspondence.

Jeffersonian methods of removal weren't as phys-
ically cruel and deadly as those of later presidents,
such as Harrison the elder and Jackson, but his underhanded plans worked. One of the nations that he
coerced into moving was the Wah-Zha-Zhi, a name

anglicized as the Osage. The Wah-Zha-Zhi were prominent in what is now the state of Missouri, but they
gave up that homeland during the Jefferson administration and eventually took up residence in Kansas,
which was then commonly known as "the Big Desert."
That, however, was before somebody figured out that
wheat would grow in "the Big Desert." Under pressure,
the Wah-Zha-Zhi left their Kansas land and bought
a huge, isolated tract in a rugged part of Oklahoma
Territory where hardly anything would grow—except
money, when oil was discovered there in about 1890.

Starting in 1906, the Wah-Zha-Zhi were awash in
money, their oil royalties from what is still known as
Osage County growing to $27 million per year. Families
such as the Tall Chiefs invested well and grew their
holdings in other businesses. Independently wealthy,
one branch of the family moved to Los Angeles for the
sake of their talented little girls, Maria and Marjorie.
With the best dance training available, they later became internationally renowned in the ballet. As money
and oil kept on gushing in Osage County, the ro-
togravure sections of newspapers all over the country
ran photographs regarded as incongruous: Indians in
native dress sitting in new Rolls-Royce roadsters or
limousines, up to the hubs in mud and surrounded
by oil fields as far as the eye could see. In actuality,
it was no more a mismatch than the specter of any
other nouveau riche Americans turning compulsively
to British luxury goods, but the sight of rich Indians
was unbearable for a certain strain of Americans, who
descended on the Wah-Zha-Zhi. The most predictable
of them put on clean clothes, sat for a neat haircut, and

then went in search of a spouse. The worst did that, married into the Wah-Zha-Zhi, and then conspired to commit multiple murders in order to inherit family fortunes. In between were hundreds of schemes to cheat Indians through slick deals, one-sided contracts, and wildly overpriced fancy goods. Considering that local officials exerted no concerted effort to stop the murders (and were in some cases compliant with them), the cheaters were even safer, effectively encouraged by local officials to knock the Wah-Zha-Zhi back down to a shadow existence.

The federal government was compelled to step into what was being called the "Osage reign of terror," first by setting the nascent Federal Bureau of Investigation (FBI) to work investigating the murders, and second by assigning special advisers specifically to protect the Indians from cheaters. The FBI acquitted itself well, though even it was overwhelmed by the breakdown of civilization in Osage County. In the most shocking of many violent cases, a white rancher was arrested for masterminding events in which he married off his nephew to a Wah-Zha-Zhi woman before arranging for the murder of her and her family. A nearby newspaper ran a feature in the wake of the white rancher's 1924 arrest, focusing specifically on his saddened wife and daughter and remarking that "In all the confused welter of events during and after the Osage 'reign of terror,' there are no more tragic figures than these two women."

That report stands as a record of the prevailing attitude in Osage County. Wah-Zha-Zhi Indians had been vaporized in explosions, beaten, poisoned, and shot execution-style for the sake of oil money, but that wasn't so very tragic, according to the local newspaper. A murderer's wife and daughter had to run Dad's ranch.

On the level of cheating, as opposed to felony criminal activity, advisers appointed on the state or local level took on the reign of *error*, in the welter of which cheaters talked Osage Indians into making irreversible financial mistakes. Six hundred such advisers succeeded in an unfortunately appropriate way. First, they charged a fee for making sure that their client Wah-Zha-Zhi weren't fleeced. It worked out to 93 percent of the oil royalties held in trust. To make sure that vile cheaters couldn't make off with the other 7 percent, the advisers had to be thorough—and they usually were, absconding with $8 million between about 1921 and 1924. Vagabond cheaters packed up and left, but the appointed ones stayed, until 1925, when they were summarily fired or held in check by emergency federal legislation.

The 1920s were a long time ago, of course, and it's heartening to think that no one takes advantage of Indians in a wholesale way anymore, especially not the Wah-Zha-Zhi. It's always heartening to look back on the coarse behavior of people in the old days, before modern thinking inculcated a finer sense of humanitarian values. The Koch family, which came into a fortune during the Oklahoma oil boom, weren't specifically involved with Wah-Zha-Zhi oil then, but they would be. By the 1980s, Koch Industries boasted of being "the largest gatherer of crude oil in the country." The company transported oil through the Midwestern regions of the United States, as well as Canada, refining much

of it at its own facilities. It was the single biggest purchaser of oil from Wah-Zha-Zhi land in Oklahoma. In
the late 1980s, other companies, including Conoco, Sun
Oil, and Philips, also bought oil from the nation, the
main difference being that they paid for what they took.

Koch Industries used a special system for the Wah-
Zha-Zhi wells, underreporting the amount of oil
pumped—and so the amount that the company owed
the Indians. In one year, 1985, it neglected to mention
1 million barrels. One might chalk up their filching to
the rough-and-tumble world of the oil industry, a constant melee that puts the "wild" in wildcatting...and
besides, life isn't fair and business is king. One might
also argue, as Koch did, that rough estimates are always
used in crude oil purchases and they aren't expected
to be perfectly accurate—except that by some statistical
anomaly, the inaccurate Koch estimates were invariably
found to cheat the Indians. In addition, Koch tended
to pay its non-Indian oil suppliers honestly; not always,
but usually. When a Senate select committee led by
an outraged John McCain began an investigation and
sent associates to Oklahoma to check Koch oil mea-
surements of Wah-Zha-Zhi oil, it seemed as though the
1920s had never ended.

The select committee's final report presented evidence that "Koch Oil, the largest purchaser of Indian
oil in the country, was engaged in a widespread and so-
phisticated scheme to steal crude oil from Indians and
others through fraudulent mismeasuring and reporting." The part of the report that really smacked of nos-
talgia, however, was the response of government agents
on the scene in Oklahoma, working for the Bureau of

Land Management (BLM): "While BLM Oklahoma officials acknowledged that Indian land was 'wide open' to massive oil theft such as the committee uncovered, they admittedly did nothing to detect it." If only the officials had read more history, it would have occurred to them to charge the Wah-Zha-Zhi a fee of 93 percent for protection of that quality.

That was the 1980s, though, back when people were coarse, when they weren't looking out for others, when diversity began and ended with watching, teary-eyed, while a Cherokee princess named Pale Moon sang the "Star Spangled Banner" at a political convention. It was a moving moment for those present, a Cherokee princess who loved America enough to sing an old English ditty with added lyrics about a battle.

There is no such thing as an Indian princess, however. "Pale Moon" was a fraud who made a fortune representing Indian causes. She wasn't a Cherokee or any other kind of Indian, but that was the 1980s—a decade that bestowed writing awards on Jamake Highwater, another fake Cherokee who became rich speaking out against the cynical mendacity that marked the treatment of Indians.

At the same time, Elizabeth Warren was presenting herself to Harvard University as being part-Cherokee, part-Delaware, a claim for which there was no written proof.† In 2017, she undertook to have her background

---

† Donald Trump was then inspired to call her by the name of a Mattaponi/Pamunkey Indian woman, Pochahantas, who deserves better than to have her name become a term of Trump's oafish mockery. n.b. "Pochahantas" was not her given name, but a pet name bestowed on her by a loving father.

traced genetically, resulting in one analyst's conclusion that she was between 1/64th and 1/1024th American Indian. Legally, a person with 1/32nd or more Indian blood is deemed Indian. A proportion of 1/1024th is less convincing. At some point, going that far back into one's ancestry, one is legally an amoeba and eligible for benefits accordingly. There is no direct indication that Warren benefited from her Cherokee/Delaware heritage, whatever its level, but she may have.

Throughout academia, prospective students present themselves as American Indian when they aren't, in order to receive scholarships so designated. Applicants for jobs do the same thing. To name just two instances, a Native American studies professor at the University of California–Riverside was widely rebuked for her unsupported claim to be a Cherokee, while a newly named administrator of Native American studies at Dartmouth College couldn't stay in the post after her alleged Delaware heritage was disputed.

The reader will no doubt be relieved to hear that I am not a faux Cherokee. Or a designer Delaware. The twisting angles of cheaters who impersonate Indians are hard to wrack into a complete shape. The problem it presents hangs in midair like a torn trapezoid. In order to get ahead, people check "Indian" as their ethnicity, taking up seats and leaving fewer chances for actual members of Indian nations; then the cheaters often get rich. Most leave it at that, but some, as the final anomaly, speak out on behalf of impoverished Indian people—with pity masquerading as pride.

While fake Indians were being heard at conventions and in many college classrooms, the case against Koch

Industries was blocked from further congressional action, as well as from criminal court through intervention from Senator Bob Dole and other political figures connected to the two Koch brothers who owned the company. No one, however, could stop another brother, Bill, from suing the company under the False Claims Act. His contention was that he would have received more money for his stake in the company had it not been for the falsified oil purchases. The case stretched on for the better part of a decade. In 1999, a jury finally found the company guilty. Naturally, Bill Koch spent that day celebrating. Mr. Koch, who was worth an estimated $850 million, had reason to be happy; as a result of the verdict, he was due to receive mad money in more ways than one, being assigned one-third of the $25 million penalty assessed from his brothers' company. The government would receive the other two-thirds. "The Osage," said Bill Koch's attorney, "won't get a penny of this money."

In hockey terms, Koch Industries cheated against the Indians (score 1) and then Bill Koch went into the net and tossed out the puck, so that the government could cheat them again (score 2). If it were hockey, it would have gone down in history.

Fortunately, modern Americans can rest easy. The Koch verdict was returned in an ancient millennium. Historians note that back in 1999, people were coarse and insensitive by today's standards. They were shallow, perhaps because they didn't stream gritty shows about minorities. As the value of oil increased in the 2010s, cheaters raced right past Osage County, Oklahoma. They were headed for the western part of

North Dakota, where the Fort Berthold Indian Reservation lay in the middle of a mammoth underground shale deposit. Occupied by the Mandan, Hidatsa, and Arikara (MHA) Nation, the land officially belonged to the federal government, unlike the Wah-Zha-Zhi land in Oklahoma. While the boom was on all around the impoverished reservation, drilling on tribal land awaited the long process of government approval. In the meantime, MHA members made money in trucking services and supplying water to oilfields in operation beyond their borders. Or so it seemed. Outside companies forced many MHA counterparts under by "fronting," or bringing massive assets to market under the name of a single tribal member. In the rush to front, cheaters like twenty-eight-year-old James Henrikson descended on MHA businesses. Originally from Washington State but arriving from Texas, he was a slick guy with a fashionable fiancée and they wowed Fort Berthold. The two formed a trucking partnership with Tex Hall, the chairman of the MHA nation.

People could get into a lot of trouble listening to James Henrikson. In anticipation of bigger plans, he fathered a baby with Hall's teenaged stepdaughter, dumped his wife, became engaged to the stepdaughter, and came close to absorbing Hall's mineral rights (worth hundreds of millions of dollars, depending on the price of oil). In the hellbent race to cheat for a fortune on the reservation, he was far out in front of the pack.

Unfortunately, Henrikson had two qualities that are detrimental to good cheating. He was impatient, which is dangerous. And he was a sociopath, which is distracting. It's actually distracting to all concerned, except—or especially—for those killed. Henrikson suddenly began to rush his fate by making people disappear or by having them shot in cold blood by hired hitmen of his acquaintance. The police arrested him when he was said to be on the verge of murdering Hall. Henrikson was sentenced to two consecutive life sentences.

Rampant cheating on the Fort Berthold Reservation revved up into the daily expectation of crime. Fortunately, the chaotic degradation of life for the MHA Indians was a long time ago: this year.

CHAPTER 4

Rooked but Good

The proper way to respond to getting cheated

An apology ceremony on live TV in America was the stuff of family life in the early 2000s. When the politician/adulterer was taking his place at the microphone, we in the TV audience had only a few seconds.

Quickly, quickly. We skimmed through the faces behind the politician/adulterer, a ragged coterie of aides, lawyers, and crisis managers. Even as the director's finger descended on the button for the close-up, our eyes were glued stage left. That's the spot for the wife.

As soon as TV screens across America switched to the tight close-up on the politician/adulterer, the audience settled back for the main event. We knew enough to ignore any and all references to little children, puppies, kittens, snowmen, and chocolate chip cookies, or anything else warm from the oven. And we knew by rote the words that lay bare the politician/adulterer's soul, revealing emotions straight from his heart.

"This chapter was a small but painful part of the past in an otherwise wonderful marriage..."*

And that means: *My favorite year.*

"The remorse I feel will always be with me..."†

That means: *It wouldn't happen again, if I could figure out how I got caught.*

"I would secondly say to [my wife], anybody who has observed her over the last twenty years of my life knows how closely she has stood by my side in campaign after campaign, in literally being my campaign manager and ... in a whole host of other things throughout the lives that we've built together..."‡

That means: *Anybody want her?*

"I want to thank my colleagues in the House of Representatives, Democrats and Republicans alike. They come from different places around the country, but fundamentally we all agree. They're all patriots and I will miss them all. Thank you..."§

---

* Representative Bob Livingston (R-Louisiana), withdrawing from his imminent post of Speaker of the House, after admitting to affairs, despite being a husband and father, December 18, 1998
† Governor Elliot Spitzer (D-New York), resigning with apology for patronizing a prostitute, despite being a husband and father, March 12, 2008
‡ Governor Mark Sanford (R-South Carolina), resigning with apology for having an affair, despite being a husband and father, June 24, 2009
§ Representative Anthony Weiner (D-New York), resigning with apology for sending obscene pictures of himself to an underage girl, despite his being a husband and father, June 16, 2011

That means: *You're up here next.*

"My thoughts and prayers..."

That means: *I wonder if there are any more olives in the back of the refrigerator.*

"...are with all those affected by my actions."

The onion-stuffed ones go good with Beefeater's, but all we have left as I recall is Tanqueray.

"I really do send them my thoughts and prayers today."

I really do wonder if there are any more olives in the back of the refrigerator.

That done, the politician/adulterer turns away from the microphone. Across America, the TV audience leans forward, en masse. And there she is! The wife, standing ramrod straight, is staring forward into the middle distance. Her husband puts his hand on the small of her back and they move away, both searching frantically for a child, any child, to take unto their bosom.

The national conversation then begins anew—not about adultery, but what each of us would charge to stand up there, on display, while our husband addressed the entire nation and explained with a pained expression that he would thenceforth make the supreme sacrifice for the sake of his children, his career, and the Statue of Liberty. He would stay home and sleep with his wife.

The response to a cheating spouse is a negotiation, but one that doesn't necessarily transpire between the two spouses. Far more often and very wrenchingly, it occurs entirely within the person who was cheated.

"I wish I were independent," said a wife and mother in Detroit. "I have been married ten years and have two children, one just a baby. The last year life has been unbearable. For years my man has gambled, but recently it is drinking and other women, as well. He is out two or three nights a week and I never know where he is. He makes fairly good money and we don't need for anything and he figures that so long as he provides for us he can go his way. He has been going about with a single girl and when I ask him to give her up, he tells me to become broad-minded.

"I wish I were independent," the Detroit wife said, "but I'm not; I have to stand it." She had chosen the first and most natural response to cheating by a husband: recrimination, loudly and often. She pulled the secret out into the open. Finding that didn't work, she wrote to a columnist at a Detroit newspaper. The year was 1932, smack in the middle of a span when novels, plays, and movies advised women in a similar position to respond by going off and having an affair of their own. Usually with Robert Montgomery, the handsome actor who played the cad-about-town in pictures of the day. The columnist didn't tell the Detroit wife to do that, but she did suggest suing for divorce with a judgment for alimony and child support.

During the Depression, divorce rates grew to record

highs and marriage rates sank to all-time lows. Financial hardship undoubtedly contributed to both, but the
dilution of attitudes toward family life was the semi-
nal influence. The worldliness or world-weariness that
marked the post–World War I years was only bolstered
by the 1929 collapse of the American economy. Many
other reasons could be blamed or credited—for example, jazz music was invariably named by those who
disapproved of the trend against marriage, while the
steep increase in college graduates was named by those
who approved of it. The confirmed bachelor or bache-
lorette was understood and accepted. Such people had
no great use for a family or a spouse. On the subject
of liaisons or relationships, or a becalmed lack thereof,
they wanted to do just as they pleased.

You may well be complicit with an insidious form
of coercion, one you would no doubt deny. If you have
ever found yourself wondering why some thirty-year-
old person in your circle has never been married or
in a long-term relationship—or in any known relationship—then it follows that deep down, you think
that everybody should be with somebody, and for life.
If ever you uttered the words, "I wonder what's up
with that," about the thirty-year-old's solitary lifestyle,
then you are marked. You are an agent provocateur of
cheating.

By some means not yet studied, the thirty-year-old
in question will be aware of your conversation. A
decade or so of such side glances coaxes single people
to slide toward marriage, whether they are good candidates for it or not.

This juxtaposition of friends as captors is the subject

of the 1970 Stephen Sondheim musical *Company,* which shows a thirty-five-year-old swinging bachelor named Bobby resisting the pressure to find one woman and marry her—until the very last song, in which he realizes that settling down with one person is "Being Alive." That's a profound observation, except for that other type of single person for whom the same song would be titled "Being Suffocated Practically to Death." Sondheim could make it scan. At the height of the Free Love Era, 1970, the discussion of an unmarried life was of interest, but nonetheless, the conclusion was that Bobby had to have a wife.

In the realm of marital cheating, the years from about 1928 to 1938 offered a glimmer of a difference. People who didn't want to be tied down were under less pressure than at any time before or since. The man-of-the-world bachelor or the independent-minded single woman were regarded as intriguing, rather than dubious. If one liked to play the field a little or maybe a lot, one didn't marry. That logical alternative to the acceptance of a covenant that cannot be kept eventually inspired a backlash. Understandably, the undermining of family life by the Depression was addressed, with focused efforts in churches and in the press and by trendsetters to bolster stability in the home. With those efforts returned the humming suspicion of anyone who "wanted to do as they pleased" romantically. In the decades since, those sorts of people were more likely to give in and get married. In time, when their spouses were betrayed, the advice those spouses heard from respectable people changed, too. It was flint hard and no longer included having a revenge affair with Robert Montgomery.

In 1977, a woman calling herself "Boiling and Miserable" wrote to columnist Ann Landers. For thirty years, she had enjoyed what she described as a "beautiful" marriage. Then she received an anonymous letter revealing that her husband was having an affair with an acquaintance (to be called Glenda, though that is not necessarily her real name). Glenda was also married, with a teenaged son. Boiling and Miserable had a ready response to the cheating. She wanted "to go to the woman's husband and tell him what's been going on. I believe it would be very effective if his wife and my husband were confronted head-on by both him and me."

Boiling and Miserable was choosing to respond materially. She didn't want a divorce. She wanted to exert power in her own right, without resorting to the protection of the courts. That wasn't a widely accepted response. "Do you want to end your marriage and create a gigantic stink?" Miss Landers wrote tartly in reply. "If so, your plan would surely do it." In view of Boiling and Miserable's feeling that "I am beside myself with anger at having been betrayed," a big stink might have been exactly what she yearned for. Presuming that the marriage was to be saved, Landers continued: "Wait until the rage subsides, then decide whether you want to talk to him—privately—or remain silent and hope the affair dies of natural causes." The advice of forbearance and turning a blind eye to infidelity was a stock answer for Landers. Remarkably, she had been in much the same position as Boiling and Miserable two years before.

Landers considered that she, too, had a beautiful marriage, with her husband, Jules, a principle owner of Budget Rent A Car. This book steers clear of most celebrity cheating for good reason: when Jules was spending almost all of his time between 1972 and 1975 in England, Landers chalked it up to their jet-set, borderless, money-drenched way of life. In 1975, he told her that he had been having an affair over the past three years with a woman twenty-nine years his junior. It beggars belief that she hadn't heard about it from her fellow jet-set, borderless friends, many of whom socialized with Jules in London, but whether or not she remained silent, the affair didn't die of natural causes. One regrets to hear of the heartache that ensued for Landers. She should have written to Boiling and Miserable for advice. As it turned out, Landers didn't take her own usual counsel in the wake of Jules's admission, announcing within twenty-four hours her plans to divorce.

The advice for the wife to stay as quiet as a mouse in the face of infidelity was typical of Landers and indeed most other such commentators, both professional and amateur, during a long era in America. That advice is still quite common, but when it was the standard in American society at all levels, the reverse was not at all true. The "unwritten law" held that a husband could defend his marriage, meaning that if his wife were having an affair, he could respond by killing the lover and possibly even the wife. The unwritten law was held up as a warning to stray tomcats. It also could play an unofficial factor in prosecution, depending on the disposition of the prosecutors.

The specter of the cheating wife was considered an

anomaly for most of the twentieth century, a darkly sur-
prising one. The fact that nearly as many wives commit
adultery as husbands has been quantified by studies
since the 1950s and by anecdotal research before that.
In one of the shifts in the attitude toward cheating, it
has become accepted as an equal-opportunity proposi-
tion over the last quarter-century, and adultery by wives
has lost its shock value. Early in the last century, a New
Jersey woman with twelve children at home was suspected by her husband of having an affair. Before long,
he caught her with a local man in a hotel room, but he
didn't shoot her. He had her arrested, either for adultery or perpetual motion. The story of the adulterous
mother of twelve, which we can later pitch to Hollywood as *Cheaper By the Dozen*, was newsworthy in 1907.
The point of recounting her affair is probably that it is
still newsworthy today, but inasmuch as there are people in every era who are not cut out for marriage, it
seems counterproductive to advocate for it as a stabiliz-
ing factor in society, or in the life of one person.

Consider the following:

"K." A man, forty-five. Has three kids from two
marriages and is known to be a little less than
loyal to the second wife.
"B." A man, forty-five. No children, never married,
has girlfriends, some last longer than others.

Which of the two is more likely to be nominated for
town justice in the next election? Principal of the local
school? Trustee of the bank?

It will be K, of course. He is regarded as the man

who has settled down, even when the exact opposite is true. And in a year or so, on a summer night when B is tearing into a steamy rack of ribs with his latest conquest at a local restaurant, across town, K's wife is tearing into a hotel room where K has checked in with his latest conquest. The court, the school, and the bank may reconsider the specter of a kind of stability that turns out to be anything but.

In cases of monetary cheating, where the amounts are small, the experience of seeking justice may only add to the angst. Even if the court finds against the cheater, it is typically incumbent on the cheated person to collect the award. And if that were easy, there wouldn't have been a case in the first place.

In larger court cases regarding cheating, the process is likely to be just as frustrating, because people who have been cheated don't—as a general rule—have as much money as people who cheat. In a civil case, the legal fees can be high and the defense strategy is often to stretch the case out into years. One such case was a milepost in the development of intellectual property law, but that was nothing compared to its importance to the widow of a Connecticut actor who had branched out by collaborating on a new play. When he died in the middle of the project, his coauthor stole his work. In an irony that makes the writers of books on cheating euphoric... the title of the play that was plagiarized was *Cheating Cheaters*.

I've been waiting for four chapters to tell you that.

Cheating Cheaters was first staged the year before America entered World War I and it has been around ever since, its story imparting a message of cheating as modern as tomorrow. The plot, presented as a "comic drama," centers on a family of cheaters who pretend to be rich, as they worm their way into the good graces of a well-heeled family. They plan to con their new friends out of a fortune. In Act II, the rich family of easy marks turns out to be yet another family of cheaters, who are themselves scheming to rip off the first family! The only honest entry in the whole dramatis personae is the leading lady, who is in reality a police detective only pretending to be a cheater, so that she can arrest the rest of them as the curtain falls. The play was a big hit, running a year on Broadway and crisscrossing the country for twenty-five years after that, before being immortalized on the screen in two different movies. *Cheating Cheaters* was a goldmine.

In reality, the law descended on the producer, who apparently failed to see the comic possibilities in the fact that his playwright, Max Marcin, had cheated his way into *Cheating Cheaters*. A young screenwriter who knew Marcin at about the same time and worked with him successfully said that he was "a wizened, wiry little fellow with keen, cunning eyes. Selfish and opinionated, he spoke the language of the executive elite."

Marcin could probably write, though he didn't, as his publicity claimed, win "a $10,000 short story contest against competitors like Rudyard Kipling and Jack London." In fact, he came in eighth in the writing contest, behind the kind of fiction writers who had three names and short-lived fame—no Kipling, no London.

Many of Marcin's stories and plays were about impoverished people becoming suddenly rich. The same could be said of works by an actor named Byron

Ongley, who was the author of the hit play *Brewster's Millions*. When Ongley came up with an outline for a play he called *Birds of a Feather*, he easily sold it to the biggest producer in New York, his good friend and colleague Al Woods. Then he asked Marcin to join him, specifically to add snappy dialogue, the two of them signing a contract covering the partnership. Their work was well along when Ongley traveled to Wilmington, Delaware, to try out a different play that he was directing. Opening night there was so exciting, members of the company stayed up late afterward to plan the triumphant New York premiere the following week.

At dawn, the porters at the Hotel du Pont, where the company was staying, heard a thud outside. Ongley had fallen out the window of his guestroom on the third floor. Detectives identified the cause of the accident as Ongley's having stumbled just as he opened the window, which seems a very difficult bit of stage business even for a seasoned actor, it being hard to open a large window without having both feet planted on the floor. However it happened, young Mr. Ongley was gone.

Marcin and Woods lost no time in coming up with a new title for *Birds of a Feather* and apparently *Cheating Cheaters* came easily to mind. The play opened on Broadway in 1916 and while no one mixed it up with *Macbeth*, which was running down the street at another theater, or *Six Who Pass While the Lentils Boil*, the surprise hit of the season, the play was very well-liked. Not loved, but well-liked. One of Ongley's contributions, the surprise that both families were crooked, was a winning plotline. His idea to make the triumphant detective a woman charmed audiences. Many, many audiences.

Mrs. Amy Ongley was incensed. The only thing worse than someone you know enjoying a major hit is someone you know enjoying a major hit with your late husband's material. She was hardly a powerhouse, however, pulling together a living for herself and her small daughter by playing small parts in plays around New York. The odds of her successfully suing a big producer such as Woods and an aggressive man such as Marcin were long, since New York courts were notoriously unsympathetic in plagiarism squabbles, especially those stemming from the theater. Mrs. Ongley, however, was fortunate in that Martin Littleton Jr., a "suave and cool" Brooklyn lawyer, took her case on a contingency basis. Regarded as something of a socialite, he may well have known Ongley, who was a popular clubman in town.

Marcin and Woods, in turn, hired Nathan Burkan and Max Steuer, respectively, to defend their rights to the profits. Though the two were not partners they were described as "the town's foremost criminal lawyers." Burkan had a lifelong interest in what is now called intellectual property law. Having been instrumental in founding the American Society of Composers, Authors and Publishers (ASCAP), he was passionate that artists be paid for their work. In the Ongley case, though, he would be passionate that they weren't. He probably took Marcin's side in part for the chance to oppose his rival, Steuer, in court and also because he was a bon vivant. Marcin had the money to pay a large retainer.

Mrs. Ongley filed a suit for $50,000 (equivalent to about $1 million in today's dollars). What eventually became *Ongley v Marcin* flip-flopped through twelve years of hearings, the opposing sides clutching like two exhausted boxers, refusing to quit. In 1927, it was over. Mrs. Ongley won. And then, in 1929, it was over again, this time for good, thanks to the state's highest judicial body, the Court of Appeals. Mrs. Ongley's side lost.

Many law students today are aware of the Nathan Burkan Memorial Award and vie for the prizes it distributes for the best essays submitted on copyright issues. Herewith is my essay for the contest, although I'm not in law school:

Mr. Burkan, you are a phony sack of—

Let me start over.

Mr. Burkan, you devoted your career to defending every two-bit composer who ever stole an old folk song and then wanted to collect $100,000 a year in royalties for it. (To composers: I don't blame any of you; Grieg did it, too.) But when George Ongley managed to think of a new way to get a bunch of rich-looking people onstage while making the members of the audience feel superior, you had not the slightest appreciation for his achievement. Have you ever tried to think of an original way to make rich people seem adorable onstage? Have you? Anybody who succeeds in that deserves royalty, let alone royalties.

Then in court, you made an unending—what is the word—*stink* (thank you, Miss Landers) about the fact that Ongley only finished one and a half acts out of three. Had I been of counsel that day, I would have reminded the court that one and a half acts constitutes half the play. And you continually made it sound as though Ongley was a failure because of that! First of all, as one who should know, I can tell you that it is much harder to write half a play than a whole play.

At about the halfway point, the most ardent kind of playwright, Sisyphus-like, will throw the whole thing out and start over. This becomes a way of life.

Sir, are you inferring that Ongley didn't just fall out a window at the Hotel du Pont...that maybe he was starting over? He didn't just hit the sidewalk, he got busy with other things? Do you literally believe that death is what happens when you get stuck on the second act?

In conclusion, had Ongley simply grown difficult and left the completion of the play to Marcin, either he or his widow *still* would have deserved half the profits. However, let me remind you that Ongley wasn't just being difficult. He was being dead.

May your equestrian statue in the rotunda of the Copyright Lawyer Hall of Fame denote on the base that Mrs. Amy Ongley, widow, didn't get a nickel of the money she deserved, thanks to the dogged efforts of "the father of copyright law."

In court or out, responses to cheating are generally equal in terms of efficacy, or lack thereof. To scream and screech like the Detroit housewife at least brings everything out in the open. To seek revenge like Boiling and Miserable shares the pain with the cheater. To keep silent allows for all options to remain open as long as possible. To go to court gives permanency to the record of cheating. To have the cheater arrested, if possible, gives temporary satisfaction. If the goal is substantive change, however, all are apt to fail. Convincing the cheater to return to the rules to which he or she agreed is likely to be impossible. More to the point, any response is doomed to fail when it brings the cheated person down to the level of the cheater. One must accept the philosophic enigma that true cheaters have always cheated before. There is no first time.

The cheated person cannot compete, having bumbled through life without thinking compulsively about the possibilities of the moment. The mind-set is all wrong, inflexible to a microclimate that changes every quarter second. That is not to say that a person can't come to the world of cheating later in life, but not as a result of a mental decision. You may as well *decide* to be a crocodile and then go swimming with one. Trying to out-cheat a cheater is just as sane.

At Syracuse University in upstate New York several generations ago, an opportunist sold "cribbing machines," gadgets that contained not just a few answers to tests, but all of them. During the midterm exams at the College of Applied Science, a majority of students took out the cribbing machines and got to work. On cue, five students then put their pencils down, stood up, and walked out. As they reached the door, the professor asked them what they thought they were doing. One spoke for the group, saying in an even tone that they "refused to compete against students cheating to pass the test." That was all; then they left.

The university launched what was called "a rigid investigation" and stopped the sale of the cribbing machines, along with other methods of cheating. The five protesting students were eventually commended. They didn't tarry with the cheaters. They didn't raise their voices. They didn't "tattle" or involve themselves further in the mess. *Facta non verba*—Deeds, not words. In the realm of a solid response to cheating, that also translates to gathering their marbles and refusing to play. Few actions disarm a cheater more fully than to be left behind; without words, but only the thunder of action.

CHAPTER 5

Game Change

The accommodation of the cheater

At the Westmoreland Country Club, a fashionable course near Chicago, the caddies of the early 1920s had seen it all, despite the fact that they weren't yet adults. In fact, they weren't teenagers, either. They weren't even youths. Most were ten or eleven years old.

While a modicum of child labor has merit, work being intriguing to youngsters, it's hard to picture the grown man who felt comfortable letting a ten-year-old lug his golf bag. And if such a man did exist, in endless foursomes just outside of Wilmette, it is even harder to imagine him placing his faith in the caddy's opinion of the ball's lie, with an added tip on the moisture content of the green and a reminder to choke up on the niblick for a chance at par. Caddying, however, was not particularly well-paid work. Westmoreland, try as it might, had trouble recruiting anyone at all to carry the clubs, let alone the robust Scotsmen it no doubt would have preferred. As it was, wee bairns caddied for a nominal wage and the hope of tips.

The caddies at Westmoreland may have been a gang of little guys, but they needed no Fagin to teach them. They knew the ethics of golf.

The game had arrived in America and specifically in Chicago only a generation before. With the addition of betting on friendly games, golf then took its place as the preferred way to make fresh air tolerable and exercise bearable. Cheating also became a part of a good day on the links. The old Brooklyn *Eagle*, a forthright newspaper if ever there was one, saw nothing wrong with cheating in golf and what is more, nothing remarkable about expecting the caddy to be complicit. When a caddy, noted the paper, "is the only spectator of what goes on in a trap, he does not publish his knowledge to the world. When the golfer having finally holed out turns to him and inquires: 'What did I make, caddie? Five or six?' the caddie knows enough to say 'five.'"

Needless to say, if something goes on in a trap that is worth publishing to the world, the correct answer would be more like "twelve." If not more. Everybody on the other side of the berm suspects that the golfer (the one with only one small spectator in the trap) had six hacks in the sand alone. But such a calculation is only something one *thinks* on the golf course. One doesn't say it. Certainly not if one is a caddy. The caddy, explained the *Eagle*, "always gives the golfer the benefit of the doubt."

That presumption ended with a jolt at the Westmoreland Country Club in August 1922. William P.

Kent, an officer at a large insurance company, was incensed. "Caddies have been a nuisance on the golf course," he said. "They accuse members of cheating in their scores and if the members don't come across with a five-dollar bill, they threaten to report."

It was true. "Cough up $5 or I'll tell your real score," became the caddy mantra at the club. The boys had been engaged, after all, to take part in the game of golf, not to kick balls out of the rough. Not to watch in silence as their temporary boss stepped on a ball hit badly and then walked closer to the green to drop a new ball from a hole in his pocket. Some players mixed golf with soccer, kicking the ball for distance or toeing it gently to a better lie. They became dexterous with a putter—not to stroke the ball, but to flip their marker closer to the hole. It isn't exactly golf, but a related game. When a player perfects it for the sake of ego or a steep return on a bet, the caddy who makes it all possible naturally wants to share in the victory.

William P. Kent was part of a cadre of aggressive businessmen who had left the dominant New York Insurance Company a few years before to form the North American Insurance Company, startling the conservative industry with a charter that gave them concentrated powers of governance. Kent, the secretary/treasurer, was at the hub of the successful company that resulted. He was accustomed to starting battles and winning them—until he met Charlie Bruckhauser.

"[In] the play of the club championship on Aug. 15," Kent reported, "I had a caddy named Charles Bruckhauser. I believe he is eleven years old. We got along without trouble until the last hole."

After the "trouble," Charlie was called before the country club's board of governors. His testimony was secret, but according to reports, he testified that at the end of the round, he made mention of "irregularities" in Mr. Kent's play.

"The boy," Kent said, picking up the story, "demanded that I give him a tip of $5. He said that should I refuse he'd report that I had been cheating. 'If you do, you're a damned liar,' I told him."

According to Charlie, it was at that point that Kent responded "by choking and beating me."

"If he says I touched him," said Kent, "he's not telling the truth."

The Board investigated for two weeks. The standoff at the swank country club was national news. Charlie held his ground. So did William Kent, but ultimately, he was judged to have slapped Charlie out of frustration. The penalty was suspension from the club— a calamitous reproach. He never recovered his reputation and in a decision that may have been related, he moved out of Illinois within a year. Charlie, meanwhile, was likewise banished from Westmoreland, without a reason cited. Extortion may have been one of the charges; it's a cruel form of commerce, even though its use by an eleven-year-old only burnishes the image of greater Chicago in the 1920s. The boy had tripped, however purposely, on the fact that cheating was accommodated within the universe of weekend golf.

More recently, a player from Galveston, Texas, commented on that lurking reality. "The vast majority of golfers are strictly honest. The one or two percent of cheaters stand out like a wart on a beauty's chin," he railed. "Do I cheat at golf? Of course not. The only time I do is when I am almost sure that I won't be caught."

In respect to the phenomenon, the Westmoreland Country Club was not unusual, except as the venue for one of the most vivid confrontations in American history: *Kent v. Bruckhauser*. One was brawny, rich, and practiced in the ways of the world. The other was a scrawny urchin with a bemused look in his eye: a disparate match-up, even in sporting America. Charlie was eleven when he laid waste to Kent. It was the power that glows around cheating that brought Kent down, after the kid had succeeded in swiping it away from him.

Another factor in the tacit acceptance of at least some cheating in the world of golf is an invention called "client golf," also known as "boss golf." The idea in either one is to cheat such that you *lose*. That makes the other person feel good—which automatically makes them want to improve your career. I have never found it to work. Quite the opposite, but then I never had to cheat in order to lose a golf game.

Nonetheless, if you look closely on the average fairway, half the caddies are kicking a ball out of the rough and half of them are kicking a ball into the rough. "Everybody cheats" is the usual explanation for the *irregularities* in golf. While it isn't quite true that everybody cheats, the accommodation of the art by opponents on the golf course is what is striking. No such wink-wink exists in tennis, which can be regarded as boxing without the blood spatter.

The server who announces "advantage in" when the

score is really "ad out" is next going to hear a clarion voice saying, "I don't think so!" from the other side of the net. And if the expected response of "Right, right, right!—you're right!" is not instantaneous, then the server will be treated to a meticulous history of every point in the game. "You had one go over the fence into the next court and then you double-faulted, then your two unforced errors, then you tried to play the net and hit yourself in the eye." Server: [interrupting either out of boredom or abject depression] "Right, right, right. You're right." Part of tennis is that opponents invariably remember the points better than you do.

FIG. 5.1—Variance in the Accommodation of Cheating in Golf and Tennis

	Tennis	Golf
OUT-OF-BOUNDS	Cheater calls opponent's ball "out," when it is clearly in.	Cheater's ball, which was hit into the forest, is found on the fairway.
	Opponent's Response:	*Opponent's Response:*
	"You sure? Let me come over and look. Right there! Right there—that's a fresh scuff— You will if you look through my magnifying glass, it looks like dye and yes! I see fibers.	"It must have ricocheted. I'll be darned."

	Tennis	Golf
	I have a test-kit in the car, if you want to . . . Good enough, we'll call it 'in.' My point."	
FAULTS	**Cheater is serving from a point in front of the baseline.**	**Cheater tees off in front of the tee markers.**
	Opponent's Response:	*Opponent's response:*
	"You might want to check those foot faults over there! . . . Aren't they the same size as your old sneakers? I have an electric eye in the car, if you . . . Okay, good, double fault. My point."	"How 'bout that? You're on in one!"
GIMMES	**The cheater dives for the ball, just barely managing to launch a lob. Seeing that it's going to be long, the cheater screams and pretends to suffer a stubbed toe and then, distracted by so much magnificent acting, suffers a broken neck and dies instantly.**	**The cheater gauges an uphill chip shot, taking aim on the pin fifty-five feet away, before suddenly scooping up the ball, saying, "Oh, just call it one. Put me down for an eagle."**

	Tennis	Golf
	Opponent's Response:	*Opponent's Response:*
	My point.	"Good on you. Got to speed up the game"

In stock car racing, remarkably enough, no one ever cheats. "We were just trying to get a little edge," explained a car owner who had just been accused of sneaking a banned fuel-cooling device into his car. With everyone just trying to get a little edge, stock car racing is a veritable think tank for cheating, in style and strategy. Because stock cars are anything but stock, the cars are tightly regulated as to the improvements that can be inculcated. That only inspires the aggressive mechanics who are attached to the sport. More than merely accommodating shortcuts, the general atmosphere holds brilliant cheating in high regard. "In other parts of the country," lamented a Southern sports fan, "where auto racing ranks in esteem a cut above snowmobile racing and a notch below indoor soccer, a lot of people must be laughing at NASCAR. 'How,' they must be wondering, 'can a sport's governing body convict somebody of cheating and still allow the victory to stand?'" The governing body allows it because the fans allow it; and they allow it, in part, because it's the stuff of genius.

Before a Daytona 500, race officials strongly suspected that engineer Smokey Yunick had equipped his
Pontiac with a gas tank that would hold more than the
twenty-two gallons allowed. They dismantled the fuel
system, completely removing the tank and measuring
it; then they peered into the length of the underside,
hunting for secret gas tanks. Finding nothing, they left,
giving Yunick permission to roll the car back to his
shop and get it ready for the race. Muttering "I told you
so," or words to that effect, Yunick picked up the empty
gas tank and put it behind the driver's seat. Then, as
soon as the officials were well out of sight, he slid behind the wheel, started the engine, and drove away.

The inspectors weren't always supposed to be
fooled. They looked through a car built by Fred Lorenzen, a prominent driver in the 1960s, and caught him
red-handed with a twenty-three-gallon tank. That was
one gallon more than was permitted. It seemed absurd
for such an experienced driver to be trying to sneak
an obvious cheat through the last inspection before the
race. But he did. While the officials watched, Lorenzen removed the tank, putting it aside. They moved on
to the next shop, and then he installed a twenty-eight-
gallon tank in his car.

The beauty of Lorenzen's scheme was that he purposefully inoculated himself. He didn't invent that
technique, but he perfected it. The same strategy is
used by cheaters who allow themselves to be caught for
an inconsequential, one-gallon offense, or in the case
of a compulsive flirt, a slew of them. After that, they
evade suspicion on the six-gallon cheating.

Weight regulations in NASCAR races prohibit lightweight cars. Mechanics, however, learned to build light cars and then fill the fenders and other cavities with buckshot. As a race got underway, hundreds of pounds of shot then dribbled unnoticed out of the car and onto the track. Had the mechanics used stone dust, rather than buckshot ammunition, they might never have been found out, but in any case, the cars met the regulations at the start of the race.

Such schemes introduce a rarified specialty: dynamic cheating. When the race itself changes the car from clean to dirty, in relation to the rules, then invisible forces are complicit with the cheater, who is safely hidden by the sequential action. In another example from stock car racing, mechanics circumvented the rule on suspension, which mandated that cars sit high—like a *stock* car from an auto dealership. In order to make it sit low, like a race car from Italy, they would freeze the springs of their stock car just before the start. After being packed in dry ice for a few hours, the springs kept a nice, high arc and held the car aloft for the sake of inspectors. Once the race started, the springs heated up and the car sank ever closer to the track. In auto racing, a dynamic form of cheating was impossible to catch before the race (unless the inspector happened to suffer frostbite while examining the chassis).

In a similar vein, a woman in Las Vegas used to wander around casinos, looking for a certain type of electronic slot machine, in order to stand near it for a few minutes. Shortly after she left, her husband would happen by, sit down at the slot, and reap endless jackpots. The trick was that she was carrying a powerful magnet, which disabled the control system in the nominally random machine, causing it to consider every spin a winner. Her magnet initiated the first part of the sequence; in the second part, the machine's electronics faltered, due to the reaction started by the magnet; in part three, the husband played the machine, which no longer generated random winners. It paid every time.

The only problem with their scheme was that the magnet necessary to cheat the machine weighed seventy-five pounds. For those now planning to walk around in a casino carrying such a magnet, the following is a list of seventy-five-pound items that can be used in training:

Three cinder blocks
A bag of cement
Four large bags of dog food
Forty plates of spaghetti and meatballs
A 60-inch television
A dinette set
A sheep

Put any of those items in an over-the-shoulder bag, freeze a casual smile on your face, take a hike through a casino the size of an airport runway, and you will be ready. The monetary return for going through life lopsided may be tempting, however. The woman who cheated the slots with her husband reaped hundreds of thousands of dollars a year. She started the sequence, the laws of electromagnetics did the brain work, and her husband cashed in. Because she did nothing but walk around, the chances of her being caught were low.

In a related type of dynamic cheating, students cribbing for a test would write pertinent facts on a set of sugar cubes. Once the information had been used or when a proctor happened by, the cheaters would eat the evidence or else plunk it into a cup of coffee. It was an admirable contingency with its two-stage construct, yet perplexing. In high school, I was arguably the worst chemist ever to come down the pike. I didn't believe in chemistry. Some people today, with a similar gravitas, don't believe in global warming. Nonetheless, it was easier to learn the pluses and minuses of the elements than to write them on a sugar cube. For one thing, with the cubes rattling around in my pocket, a grain of sugar might fall off the "O" for oxygen, turning it into a "U" for uranium. In the middle of the test, I'd blow up the state. But this is a book about other people and their version of dynamic cheating. Apparently, the cubes were well-regarded by those who knew them to work.

Back in the master class of stock-car cheating, inspections are also conducted after the races. The controversial aspect of *just trying to get a little edge*, or cheating, in NASCAR races, however, is that cars that flunk post-race inspections can actually retain their standing. Richard Petty won a race and kept his victory even though his engine and tires were entirely disallowed afterward. The same thing has happened to a long roster of famed race teams through the years.

"You've got to cheat to win in NASCAR," was the attitude among car owners, nearly all of whom uttered those same words at some point or other. When the winning car in a NASCAR race near Los Angeles was found to have an impermissible engine, the car's owner claimed it was just a mistake. "They always say that," grumbled an official. The car retained the victory, of course.

"It was a very gray area," insisted a member of the pit crew for the car. That much was true.

Cheating thrives in the gray area. It clings to misunderstandings and depends on them to show the way. It looks for vagaries and introduces at least a few, where none can be found. So it is that wizard mechanics who can blueprint an engine in the dark or translate a rulebook into metal and then back again into paper and ink could rely on the excuse of the "honest mistake," which is inevitably hoisted up from the gray area.

For centuries, the legal world has strived to eradicate every shaft of gray. The accumulation of legal precedence aligns reality with law through thousands of previous cases. Filling long shelves full of volumes, those cases specify ever more closely what each law means within the starkest possible contrast of right and wrong. In most realms, however, people actually prefer the fuzzy edges, where those opposites are harder to separate.

When race-car drivers say, almost in harmony, that "everybody cheats," they not only let themselves off the hook, but they also confirm the acceptance of cheating on the part of non-cheaters. Many also add the corollary: "You have to cheat." The system, they are saying, incorporates cheating. It works . . . fans like it . . . anyone who argues is not part of the system. By that point, the *evolved* rules, which are not necessarily written down, have already left non-cheaters behind. They have been accorded three choices: cheat, acquiesce, or leave.

The acquiescence to cheating, the general accep-

tance of it by non-cheaters, can be even more calcu-
lated. A teacher who gives a test on poetry that results
in a flurry of flunking grades is frowned on by admin-
istrators. When, on the other hand, all the students
get an A+, displaying endless insight into every son-
net ever written by the Portuguese and/or Elizabeth
Barrett Browning, happiness reigns. If the teacher ig-
nores the possibility that the students are all cheaters,
then the level of teaching appears to be stupendous.
The children go forward with glowing transcripts. The
teacher wins tenure. One might call it a form of victimless cheating.

A very different set of events led to the test, however.
Some teacher earlier in the careers of those students
didn't let them cheat when they were learning to read
well enough to consult a crib sheet. Another teacher,
sometime later, didn't let them cheat when they were
finding out what a poem was. Having learned all of that,
which was just enough to cheat, the students decided
to stop learning. With a teacher's cooperation, they're
encouraged once and for all to abandon their curiosity.
After that and long into eternity, these are the dull-eyed
people with whom I'm expected to make conversation
at picnics.

Victimless cheating, my aunt Fanny. I want compen-
sation.

The abandonment of the stigma against cheaters is a
trend in our times across every pursuit. It can be considered in a truly clinical, even sterile, way in only one,
however.

"Gramma will either be out back in the garden or
the flower beds, and Grampa will be in the workshop or

riding around the lawn on the mower," wrote a woman in Oregon, describing the daily life of her grandparents, who lived in a mobile home in Linn County. "If one is missing from the yard activities, you'll find them sitting at the kitchen table, playing solitaire. The couple keeps their well-worn Bicycle deck on the table in the lazy Susan."

Those grandparents in Linn County lived very much like J. P. Morgan almost a century before. In the Panic of 1907, Morgan, the towering figure in New York banking, took the future of the United States into his hands at the tacit invitation of the president. Over the course of three tense weeks culminating in November 1907, Morgan's becalmed preference for predictability steadied wild swings in the financial markets. Veritably commanding banks and debtors to stand in formation, he staved off the disintegration of the nation's economy. Throughout the crisis, Morgan turned to solitaire as a reflex, sorting cards instead of banks. Even during less dramatic spans in his lifetime, he played solitaire on a daily basis, hunching over a table in a posh study in his mansion on Madison Avenue.

The goal of solitaire card games is to bring order to disarray. The player organizes a shuffled deck into a rational pattern: typically four suits arranged numerically. It's a natural impulse. Most of what is considered civilization attempts the same satisfaction: organization by and according to the hand of man. Everything from naming constellations to setting the dinner table is part of the same impulse. If the human species is distinctive, it is not (as anthropologists say) because of the thumb or the cranium. Nor (as I often say) is it because we, yes we, were the ones who invented ice cream. In truth, the distinction is the result of busy little fingers sorting anything they find into like piles or straight lines. The fingers are connected to something even more intrinsic than the brain as they bring order out of chaos as perceived by the human eye. The couple in Linn County kept every blade of grass mowed to the same height and cultivated flowers in beds without other plants: a tidy tract and yet another theater in the human mind's war against all that confuses it. J. P. Morgan tidied the banking system with the same compulsion. When each was finished, they retreated in comfort to their respective neat homes and continued the fight to bring order, in the cards, in their eyes.

Solitaire is nothing more than that quest. In the 1960s, betting on it enjoyed a minor swell of popularity in Las Vegas casinos (the player put ten chips down and received one chip for every card that was in the ace piles at the end of the game). In every other case, however, the game is fascinating exactly because it is solo: no one else sees what happens, much less cares about it. Not even the kindest friend wants to hear about the ups and downs of a day playing solitaire. It matters to no one else. For that reason, cheating at the game is in a category by itself.

Many, if not most, players cheat at solitaire. When asked why they do, they don't know. And if they don't know, then who could? Isn't cheating at solitaire tantamount to bouncing a check to yourself? Solitaire cheaters reshuffle the cards they are holding; peek under the cards on the table to see the ones hidden facedown; run through their cards one at a time, instead of the requisite three at a time, and slip a helpful card into the ace piles, even if it was actually locked up by another card. Winning by such methods is an innocent enough secret, but it's also the keystone in understanding why cheating is allowed and accommodated by so many.

Sir Isaac Newton wrote in 1687 that for every action, there is an equal and opposite reaction. In light of the more recent research presented in this book, physicists now know that he meant to add an exception for cheating in solitaire, in which there is an action followed by nothing, at least in terms of any circle of society or the natural world. If the only goal is winning in a card game, then why not go the whole way and lie: leave the cards in the drawer and declare victory. In cheating, though, something real always changes, even for one person alone except for a lamp, a coffee table, and a deck of cards.

For the solitaire player who peeks and picks, the cards will be organized into proper piles at the end of *all* the games, not just a rare few. With that, the keystone emerges. In the private universe of solitaire, breaking more rules brings more order. The player who can accommodate that incongruity can easily accept that cheating is a positive thing—when seen from a certain perspective. Non-cheaters in a whole variety of pursuits seek out that perspective, in the name of some different kind of order.

CHAPTER 6

Section One Conclusion

You. The Cheated.

Certain species have evolved over a relatively short epoch to live amicably among humans. Dogs, for example, started out as wolves or coyotes, predators that would have been inclined to attack humans, if not just avoid them altogether. Slowly but surely, some wild dogs acquired the instinct to get along with people instead.

Fifteen thousand years later, if the human wants to lie down in a dark study on a beautiful day and watch a Ruth Chatterton movie, while the dog wants a sunbath outside, the dog won't storm out of the house, saying you watch too many damned old movies and should get a life, preferably in this for-Christ's-sake century. Of course not. The dog will curl up with the human on the sofa, and bathe in the blue light of the TV. As a state of affairs, it's all far removed from the stuff of coyotes. A modern dog knows exactly how to handle the unending emotional insecurities of the average human, making the minutes and the years much easier for that person. Horses and cats have also evolved over the course of fifteen millennia, becoming experts at living in the company of humans. Other types of animals have done nearly as well, changing their instincts, along with the very profile of their micro-RNA, and acclimating themselves to people. This is basic zoology: not the origin, but the destination of the species.

The question is why humans haven't similarly evolved in order to get along with humans. Not one whit. The Old Testament of the Bible, the Tripitaka, Nuliajuk oral tradition, the Zhuangzi, the Koran, the Hozhooji and virtually every other holy record that stands as an early source on human misbehavior still rings fresh today. Wars, murders, assaults, and pillage continue apace, as popular as ever. One would think that if Charles Darwin had really been on the ball, then those *Homo sapiens* drawn to street brawling would have been killed before having children and little by little, it would be safe to walk past sports bars late at night. Human biology hasn't worked that way.

Any fleck of DNA can pinpoint which part of Kamchatka one's ancestors occupied in 1502 or quantify one's propensity for hangnails, but less customized are the markers titled "ability to break the Ten Commandments"—or the "Correct Way" of the Taishang Ganying Pian or any other sincere attempt to discourage brutish impulses. Those impulses are in fact indelible, as are all of the finer traits we know as savagery. Compared to other animals, humans are cemented in their evolutionary place. For this one species, change occurs from the outside in—that is, through codes, commandments, correct ways.

The levels of complexity in the person who gets cheated are far greater than those of the cheater. They each play their parts in a battle that, as we have seen, stretches back to the dawn of civilization fifteen millennia ago. I chart the beginning of civilization in terms of this study of cheating to the inculcation of the dog, not because I like dogs, but because that event forms a line of demarcation. It depicts a measurable timeframe when evolution might have begun for the human species—but did not. Dogs changed, cats changed, horses changed, and the angry primates that we all must be kept cheating one another, same as ever. That's a discomfiting realization. And so, in place of biological evolution, humans tried their very hardest, applying to themselves moral codes. For some, it was like slapping on a soothing mud pack: after a while, it cracked and fell off. For others, the moral codes, often based on deeply felt religions, were more like sun rays that warmed them to the very bone. The dichotomy fell roughly along the lines of everyday cheating.

The circumstance of getting cheated is that of getting swallowed up by someone else's sense of morality. Obviously, it is an involuntary experience. One response is that of affirmed virtue: fighting back by clinging to one's own morality, right and proper, as it may be. An element of selflessness easily attaches itself to that route, and any desire to maintain one's own standards, at all costs.

Loyalty is another motivation to let a cheater get away with it. Loyalty not to the cheater, but to children or parents, to a school or college, or to any individual or organization imagined to be too fragile to withstand the disturbance of a cheating scandal. The basis is that the cheated person will absorb the pain in order to protect others. While this response is very probably well-intended, the cheated person nonetheless bene-fits. He or she is strong, is proven strong, is made strong—something. Something that will turn a point of shame into a point of pride for the one who bore the brunt in the interest of the greater good.

What is left after all those millennia and right up to the present day are the former and the latter: cheaters and those with myriad reasons not to stop them cold.

SECTION TWO

You Who Cheat

CHAPTER 7

Your Own Kind

Cheating those with whom cheater has bonded

Awoman in Florida celebrated her tenth wedding anniversary with a great guy not so long ago. They were one of the nicest couples in the neighborhood, and when a friend in their circle was deeply upset by something in her own marriage, she turned to the wife for advice. During the course of the conversation, the friend broke down and confided what was disturbing her. Her husband was having an affair. Not, actually, just one affair—a relationship consecrated by organizational planning—but a slew of assignations that fell under a lower classification. He was fooling around.

No one could say that the woman wasn't interested in her friend's problem. That would be, to clarify, the woman who had just celebrated a joyous anniversary anticipating forty more years of days and nights with her great guy, maybe even fifty years. He was a really great guy. He was also a guy with whom she had no love life, but that was something she had learned to accept.

Then she heard that her neighbor's husband was fooling around.

We who have listened to these stories know to look at them by starting at the finish. The suspense then builds backward to the beginning, which is when something essential to the marriage changed.

Feel free to read from the bottom up, but for the true suspense of marital cheating, it's better to work down, backward in chronology through to the moment when it really happened:

Last step: He left her to marry one of her friends.
Ninth step: He began to forget things, like what color her eyes were, and that surprised her.
Eighth step: They settled into their new neighborhood.
Seventh step: The two of them married quietly and moved to another city.
Sixth step: Both couples were divorced.
Fifth step: By accident or design, they were caught.
Fourth step: They decided that they wanted to be together all the time.
Third step: The clandestine meetings here and there turned into a full-fledged affair.
Second step: He was open to her indications.
First step: She gave him a call on some pretext or other. (That was the moment.)

The Florida woman took her place in the ranks of cheating spouses with the decision to call her friend's husband. That is the type of action that can't be reversed, no matter how easily it arrives. Even the consequences are secondary to that moment.

The view that in terms of cheating, *trying* to start an extramarital affair is the same as actually *diving into* one refers back to the argument of a relative of mine. He couldn't fathom the crime of attempted murder. In most jurisdictions, it carries a milder punishment than actual murder: "Just because somebody is too big an idiot to shoot straight, why should he get off easier than another crook who gets it right?" In the thin slice of intent that is cheating, whatever comes later likewise barely matters. The deed is done if the deed is begun. The fact that spouses more than occasionally get ideas is out of the purview of this analysis; it's impossible to qualify the breach of "lusting in one's heart," to paraphrase the scandalous confession of a former president—Jimmy Carter, who almost lost the nomination for the presidency when he admitted that his imagination had been at times unfaithful to his wife. He may or may not have sinned, but he didn't cheat.

Cheating is action, not thought. It occurs as soon as a spouse picks up a phone or buys a drink; gets someone alone; sends a message that could be misunderstood; takes note of any of the above indications from another person and responds in kind; opportunistically removes a wedding ring; claims to be a test pilot, spy, or industrialist or all three; pretends to be a caring person, to listen, or to sincerely hope to solve somebody else's problems, laughs at strained jokes; encourages pathetic dreams, insists that there is no such thing as a pathetic dream, and remembers the name of the other person's cat. Most of this is the stuff of any first date, but in the case of nascent adultery, it is a date with a telling flaw, because many a hopeful adulterer will also make a point of his or her own misery, claiming to be lonely or to have no love life at home, all for the benefit of someone whose business it is definitely not. If a person on a normal first date does that, the chances are good that there will be no second date. For a certain kind of adulterer, though, martyrdom is home. It's also integral to a second level of cheating, which brands most such cases. First, the typical philanderer cheats the spouse and, second, the new love interest.

The hopeful adulterer is often only 1 percent unhappy, in the overall scheme. The other 99 percent of the day, everything is great and the kids are fine. The world of adultery would be a simpler place and the advice columns would be empty if, when Person A implies that they are lonely, bored, or as the cliché goes, "misunderstood," Person B could immediately ascertain within a margin of error of 2 percent just how much of A's life really is sorely and sadly bereft. Perhaps a handheld scanner could be invented. Confusion and surprise would be avoided entirely, because the vast majority of Person Bs face a relationship limited strictly to alleviating the misery section of the adulterer's life. The affair can constitute, for example, only 3.1 percent of the adulterer's overall lifestyle. Or 8.6 percent, or whatever the particular quotient happens to be, according to the handheld scanner. The rest is likely going to be strictly off-limits, which is a relief to some of those in the isosceles end of the triangle, but it becomes a disappointment to most.

Describing the Florida woman's course in terms of

its junctures, above, we note that somewhere along the line, she and her friend's husband decided that they were soul mates. While that doesn't always happen, it puts the story into a special template: the affair that grows into something more. That is, she and her friend's husband, having clearly expressed their attitude toward the tenets of marriage, decided they had to get…married. That way, they could forsake all others again, but different others. And that's what would make it meaningful—not at long last the right spouse, but the right others.

Though the Florida woman ended up marrying the man with whom she was involved, she may not have progressed much further than the rest of the Person Bs who want to settle down. Her problem was that her second husband had an unusual attitude toward marriage, in that he regarded it as a way to meet babes. After divorcing her, he repeated history by marrying one of her friends. In any case, the Florida woman herself scored the hat trick of infidelity: (1) Cheating on her husband, (2) having an affair with a married man, and (3) getting cheated upon, when her new husband had an affair. That accomplishment was lost on her. She just wanted the lug back—and she had a better than even chance of getting him, since she was, after all, friends with his latest wife.

There are people who show no loyalty to a boyfriend or girlfriend, eyeing the halls at work for something better. And there are those who blithely step out on whomsoever they are living with. More than a few rev up their prowls to a new level after becoming engaged, right up to the eve of the wedding. Both brides and grooms are known to have a last call with somebody or other on the very eve of the wedding. Such people may be rakish and unbound—or devilishly vain. They may be slightly insane or insecure. They may even be sleazy, but they are not cheaters. After the vows, however, everything is different and here is why.

Those readers still slightly dizzied by the steps outlined on page 92 will be relieved to know that these go in chronological order:

First step: The mail arrives at your home, including a notice of insufficient funds from the bank; a summons for jury duty; and a letter from the IRS demanding even more money than you earned last year. Then your heart sinks: at the bottom of the pile is a "Save the Date" card.

Second step: In due course, the wedding invitation arrives, dictating terms.

Third step: One of the following ensues: you get all dressed up to sit outside in the sun on the hottest day of the year; you get dressed up to sit in an old barn; you go to a Halloween store to find something appropriate to wear.

Fourth step: You bring a gift to help the newlyweds set up housekeeping, even though they have been living together in a $600,000 condo for the past four years.

Fifth step: No matter what happens, how stale the cold cuts or how Euro the DJ's playlist, how ineducable the bartenders at the cash bar, you will be covered in a bloom of joy, first to last. You reminded yourself of that fact while parking the car.

Sixth step: Suavely and with an air of knowing confidence, you walk right past the seating chart. You go directly to the table on the farthest horizon, the one half-filled by the shortlist of potentially hazardous guests, the table bestilled amid all the festivities by a pall of disinterested silence, and you take the seat with your name card on the plate.

Seventh step: Just as the wedding couple leaves in a car for the honeymoon, people throughout the crowd look at their single relatives and shake their heads. "What a beautiful couple," they say loudly to them.

Last step: You hear later—a few months or a few years later—that the beautiful wife in the beautiful couple has picked up the beautiful phone on some pretext to call her friend's husband. A highlight reel of her wedding day plays in your mind. That's a whole day you'll never get back. The same can be said for the pizelle-maker. Adultery in marriage is a jagged circumstance, and with only bizarre exceptions, somebody's life is certain to be derailed by any love triangle. First among them is the wedding guest.

A new wedding tradition is long overdue. Upon receiving the invitation, the guest will agree to attend on the proviso that if either the groom or bride ever commits adultery, each and every one of the guests will receive a gift—and not just the return of the original ones, still in their boxes, dusty and unopened. Instead, before the wedding, the guests will walk around the stores at which *they* are registered, scanning all the stuff they want, should the bride or groom stray after the vows. To be serious, the future invariably holds secrets and sometimes a person does indeed meet the true and actual love of their life while still married to someone else. Such situations are at once glorious and insidious, leaving well-meaning spouses no good solution. Ah, the poetry. Oh, the angst. I understand completely and will be registered at Hermès.

The betrothed couple may balk at the new wedding tradition, asserting that "forsaking all others" is unrealistic in this day and age. Oddly enough, the word for that attitude has been the same for over a hundred years: "modern." In a Model T or a hybrid car, by telegram or Instagram, on the silver screen or 5G stream, any open arrangement has been termed "modern." No harm is left by such an arrangement, as long as both sides truly subscribe. As most stories unfold, however, only one of the spouses is modern. Deep down, the other thinks it will pass. It is a perfectly acceptable means of sidestepping the possibility of cheating, though, as long as the vows are clearly rewritten to be frank—without being too frank. That way, the wedding guests won't be aggravated later on. If the couple insists on a traditional wedding vow, however, *without* the concomitant intention to hand out presents if one or the other commits adultery, then the guest can obviously opt to stay home.

Without the new tradition, a love triangle does not *officially* include one hundred and sixty former wedding guests. Unofficially, however, it does. Adultery hurts more than just the spouse and leaves more than another nick in the institution of marriage. It makes one hundred and sixty people regret that they ever bestowed their hope on somebody else.

The even more distinctive element in the Florida woman's cheating was that she had the idea while listening sympathetically to a friend whose husband's infidelities were painful to the point of emotional torture. In a flash of inspiration, the Florida woman decided she would stomp on a friend, rather than go to *all the trouble* of playing farther afield to find a man somehow, somewhere who was interested in sex. Instead, she obliterated the bond with her friend, which is what marks her as a complex cheater.

The person who cheats a friend, or a close colleague, a teammate, a business partner, or a relative, is a special sort. For some, a special satisfaction accompanies the devastation of a friend. Simpler cheating looks beyond one's own inner circle, to the other eight billion chumps on Earth. In that way, cheaters can keep moving and yet leave themselves behind.

One summer day in a park outside New York City, a Harvard boy walked by a man dealing three-card monte—the game played on a folding tray or a corrugated box, by which the player doubles his money just by guessing which of the three cards lying facedown is the ace of hearts. The monte dealer shows all three, before turning them down and moving them around the table in a dance of hopping cards. Monte is notorious for the sleight of hand of the dealer, who can put the ace of hearts anywhere he wants, even in the player's hat—the one back home in the closet. Instead, he just hides it in plain sight on the table. A common ploy for the dealer is to lose game after game to one of the rubes who invariably pause in front of a three-card monte table. Of course, the winner in that case is almost certainly a shill, present only to encourage others to give the game a try.

The Harvard student was anything but a rube. Not only was he a senior at a renowned college, but he was also a man-of-the-world beyond it: specifically, the demi-monde of Broadway. He had observed three-card monte enough to see that the dealer in the park was sloppy. And he felt only contempt for him, an obvious cheater, systematically taking money from practically everybody who walked by. When the dealer turned away momentarily to answer a question, one of the prospective players spontaneously reached out and bent the corner of the ace of hearts. When the dealer turned back, the Harvard boy edged out the other man and put a dollar on the table. He felt guilty about it afterward. "This was a dirty deed," he wrote. "It's no use explaining that I would merely be cheating a cheater. The plain truth is that I didn't figure at all."

The student was not merely using his wits to right a wrong, nor was he particularly dedicated to making the world safe from bunko artists. He was getting a dollar by cheating a stranger, a person who didn't matter, which is a relatively simple act. Meanwhile, the Florida woman was starting an affair in her more complex way, specifically by cheating her friend—thereby turning that friend into a person who didn't matter. (The woman's first husband likewise became a nonentity.) One can be egalitarian or even downright biblical and observe that a stranger should be valued on par with a friend—or with a spouse. "The same manner to all human souls," as George Bernard Shaw put it. That is the hope and the frustration of humanitarians, who fear that, like the Harvard student, most people are honorable only to their friends. That certainly turned out to be the case with the man who bent the ace of hearts on cue, in order to help his friend win a buck off a stuck-up college boy.

Complex cheaters, for reasons of their own, are nice to anyone but their friends.

When a pair of men's Bible classes in Long Beach, California, and Kansas City, Missouri, decided to stage a contest, the goal was only to draw more adherents, especially business types who might be inspired by the challenge of notching the biggest attendance over the course of five weeks. The Long Beach Bible class was boosted by its president, who was also the mayor. The Kansas City group was attached to one of the biggest churches in the city. The competition worked and each of the classes was soon filled to overflowing. That ought to have been cause for celebration. It wasn't—quite the opposite, in fact. After week three, the head of Kansas City's class sent a lieutenant, J. W. Lingenfelter, to Southern California, explaining, "We did hear some reports Long Beach was padding the count. We instructed Lingenfelter to hire some detectives to check up."

Lingenfelter didn't hire "some" detectives; he hired twenty, and based on their reports, he publicly charged the Long Beach class with doubling their actual attendance figures. The mayor of Long Beach countered that the Kansas City class had used attendance figures from two different locales—when the rules clearly stated that the contest was for one single class only. Lingenfelter swatted back; his group couldn't help it if the class had *outgrown* the city's convention hall, forcing expansion to a satellite venue nearby. After that, the contest collapsed, with cheating revealed on both sides, and accusations splintering the Word.

Religions often end up at the vortex of irony, connected to tomcat preachers, embezzling deacons, attendance contests gone wicked—or other forms of cheating that pretty well smelt the Golden Rule. Each is overshadowed by the ultimate oxymoron, the religious war. On close inspection, however, one can wonder whether they are ever really fought over doctrine or the more usual factors of money, power, and the intrinsic human reflex of dividing every tableau into "us" and "them." In any case, religion certainly can't be faulted for the fact that people are flawed. Or that they cheat. That is like blaming the buckets for the fact that a ship is sinking. What is more intriguing is that in terms of cheating, the fault lines of "us" versus "them" belie the obvious loyalties. The Bible student businessmen competing for the attendance prize went after those who, in the viewpoint of an outsider, were their own kind. One might think that in a rational world, Mr. Lingenfelter and the mayor of Long Beach would have conferred on the best way to bloat their mutual numbers, thus proving the relevance of Bible teachings in American life. "Cheating for Jesus," to coin a phrase. "Cheating for Kansas City" was less logical, in actuality, except in the complex sense that the ultimate satisfaction lies in taking down those with whom one is bonded.

One of the most hallowed bonds in all of American history occurred in the early 1940s, when millions of people answered the call to fight World War II, long known as the "Good War." That might seem like yet another oxymoron, the war having been anything but good, being in fact hideous on a new scale. The enemy was well-defined for Americans, though, and the nation was united by strong leadership in vanquishing it, making it in that way a "good" war. To sound like a typescript for a newsreel of the era, American GIs fought hard on land, on sea, and in the air wherever the commanders sent them, from the Aleutian Islands to the Sahara Desert, to the high Himalayas to the dark waters of the North Atlantic. To sound like this book again, they also cheated one another hard and fast in all of the same places.

Gambling in the ranks goes back to the days at Valley Forge when General George Washington issued repeated orders to stop betting for money. In an encampment of privations that made life just shy of unbearable, it was gambling games that distracted soldiers, while pushing some of them over the edge of despair. Each gambling game is by its nature a universe unto itself, with its own natural laws, which understandably brings relief from even the worst of realities. To that extent, it belongs in military camps. The first of gambling's inherent laws, though, is that without money from somewhere, you can't play anymore. That is as devastating a thought for adults as for any child on a playground. You can't play anymore. Added to that is the wrenching awareness that real money has disappeared, no money being more real than *your* money.

With that, the soldier had to turn back to the demands of wartime. For that reason, gambling undercuts morale at a time when nothing is more critical to a young man or woman. And yet it is respite.

Some GIs, being inveterate gamblers, had a very plump war. After Richard Nixon was stationed as a naval officer in the South Pacific, he brought home upwards of $10,000 in poker winnings. He used it to buy a home and underwrite the law practice that would lead him into politics. My father brought home $1,000 from playing craps in the Army Air Corps in France; he lost it all in about ten minutes in another dice game his first weekend stateside. In the Army infantry, Tony Graziano of Canastota, New York, raked in $10,000 by setting up a casino/nightclub "somewhere in Germany" after the Battle of the Bulge. When his father back in Canastota heard about it, he made Tony close it down. A guy can push through a battle as tough as any on record but still dread the hell of getting his father mad.

Savvy or lucky gamblers were not the only ones in the ranks, however. The same military draft that took men from every other walk of life also rounded up master cheaters. In fact, most of them didn't even wait to be drafted. For cheaters, the war was a godsend: dupes by the boatload were delivered with money, time, and a callow desire to be worldly. Commercial houses that sold marked cards and tilted dice did a brisk business during the war, although prosecutors made well-publicized efforts to close them down. The armed services hired experts on gambling to tour bases; the Navy even engaged a card sharp named Mickey Mac-Dougall to go undercover aboard its ships in order to locate the gambling cheats. One that he found had already gone straight of his own volition. He was an old friend of MacDougall's by the name of Johnny, who had made a specialty of palming aces in poker. He had also perfected the art of slipping the card between his sleeve and his wrist, for use when needed. The soldier had other tricks as well, but that one regularly reaped big pots for him, from a revolving cast of GIs across the table, or rock or blanket or whatever the surface happened to be. Johnny's scheme made demands, one of which was that he couldn't leave the table for any reason. On a day when he had rather sloppily won every hand, rather than the more prudent "give a little, take a lot," he also allowed himself to be distracted when some of the other players took a short break for refreshments. He normally (and casually) made sure to pick up the deck whenever the game stopped for any reason. Instead, another player took the deck in hand and started counting the cards.

Johnny looked at the mountain of money at his place on the table and felt the ace edging his wrist. It was too late to slip the card back onto the table. It was too late to throw it on the floor. It was too late to strike up a conversation with the other player; he was too involved in his card count. Johnny looked at the pile of cards that had already been counted. When the total reached fifty-one, the other players were going to ask to see what was up his sleeves. That, as a later generation would say, was a no-brainer. The pile of cards was getting taller. It was too late for everything, except to reach for a sandwich, push the ace flat against the slice of ham inside and eat with gusto. Only the taste of cheating, or more viscerally, of coated cardboard, cured Johnny of palming aces against his band of brothers.

The notion of a band of brothers in combat referred first to the English at the Battle of Agincourt in France in 1415, which Shakespeare was recounting when he wrote the phrase. It has rung true ever since of a bond almost spiritual: "For he today," said Henry V to his troops in the play, "that sheds his blood with me/Shall be my brother." In the modern parlance, the phrase harkens to World War II, when such bonds were certainly forged, maybe at a greater rate than in other wars and maybe not. But even so, for a cheater, such bonds could vanish at lightning speed, even in the Good War and the Greatest Generation, for G.I. Joe and his band of brothers. One occasion worth recalling proved that the bond could come back, depending on how much else was already gone.

A Marine of my acquaintance was thrown into the step-by-step fighting on the islands south of Japan during that war. Playing cards, he had already won a wad of money from his brothers in arms, who resented it and suspected him of having bilked the entire Corps at one time or another. He didn't care. He had bilked them, but more Marines always came to him when he took out a deck. Not knowing when a new game would pop up, he carried his money roll into battle. The fighting was brutal. Seventy-five years later, his eyes still flashed a challenge, daring me to even try to imagine how it was. At one point long into the campaign, with the Japanese locked into the top of a hillside, the Marines were stuck near the bottom, hollowing out shelter where they could. Days went by. "I was the only one with paper," my friend said. "I handed those goddamned twenty-dollar bills out. Tens, fifties, all of them."

Not having the foggiest idea what he was talking about, I responded with disconnected syllables. "Whay-er? What?"

"They needed john paper."

CHAPTER 8

To Cheat or Not to Be

Who cheats?

A Midwesterner named Itchy Novak was a senior at a big college, where he could have lettered in varsity cheating. His field was the classroom, though he only rarely saw the inside of one during the school year. Novak managed to pass his tests by means of cribbing—arming himself with study material or an outright list of the correct answers. In spring of his senior year, he had his best semester ever, avoiding classes entirely.

After the courses ended, Itchy finally learned something: an actual fact. He was told that in order to graduate, he needed to pass his business class; and in order to do that, he needed an A on the final exam. Not even an A minus. Three and a half years of dedicated cheating were about to go down the drain; he couldn't crib or copy from another student, be-cause the professor had made it clear that the exam would be heavily proctored. And because the proctors would be graduate students and young members of the teaching staff, Novak couldn't expect to enlist their help. None of his many schemes had any chance of working, a private drama that only highlighted Novak's squandered chance to gain a good education. The tragic end of the story lay not with Novak, but with the certainty that somewhere, in a lingering haze of disappointment, was a young person who had been rejected by the same university four years earlier, in favor of Novak. That person just might have looked on class attendance as something less than agony and more than foolish.

Even in defeat, Novak was obligated to leave for home right after his business final, so that morning, he dressed for travel, putting on a clean shirt and a blazer. Still unsure of himself, he felt a certain inertia set in. Pausing before the storm, he took a good, hard look at himself in the mirror and was rocked by what he saw he had become.

Arriving at the exam room, where over a hundred seats had been arranged, Novak walked past them all and presented himself to the professor. "Good morning, sir," he said.

"Morning."

"I've been assigned as one of your proctors," Novak said. "Which aisles would you like me to patrol?"

The professor glanced at the well-dressed young man. He couldn't possibly have recognized him; Novak had never been to class. The professor assigned him a couple of aisles and when the seats were filled, Novak passed out exam "blue books," taking care to put one on his own perch, a desk in the back. Sometimes he sat back there casually scribbling in his book, but more often, he sauntered up and down like a good proctor, leaning in frequently to see what one student or another was writing: especially the smart students. He had to make sure they weren't cheating, after all. Near the end of the period, Novak was finished, writing his name on the front of his booklet. It was then that the professor motioned him down to the front of the classroom.

Novak left the booklet on his desk and walked as confidently as he could toward the professor, who was looking at him with interest. "Can I help you, sir?" he asked with Plasticine cheer.

"Yes, you can," said the professor. "Would you please collect the test booklets?"

Novak took the blue books from the other students, made a neat pile, put his booklet in the middle, and handed them in. "Thanks for your help, son," said the professor.

"Anytime, sir." Novak grinned. In due course, he graduated, and thus prepared, he was sprung on the business world.

In praise of cheaters, they can be made of the stuff of genius. Most people see only what is happening at any given moment, while leaders are supposed to see the road far ahead. Cheaters see all of that, near and far, along with six shortcuts to save themselves effort. In another type of world, one without rules, cheaters would go by another name. They'd be called "engineers." Where engineers find easier ways to accomplish the same end result, turning their profound sense of laziness into a virtue, cheaters are reviled for finding an easier way. The difference that keeps the two apart is that engineers make the world better for other people, while cheaters, across the board, don't.

Some of the greatest breakthroughs in every field were made by people who took a little from each side: innovation and skullduggery. Louis Pasteur pioneered microbiology, but he abjectly cheated when he treated humans for rabies. Pasteur was in the midst of working on a cure for the disease when he received a frantic appeal from the parents of a little boy who had been repeatedly bitten by a rabid bulldog. Pasteur didn't flinch, cheating the rules of medical science at that time (or the current one) by administering his experimental compounds without proper testing or review. A few weeks later, the boy was healthy and Pasteur was hailed a hero internationally. That particular shortcut is part of the glory of the man; he was fearless, he was single-minded, and in the wake of his dramatic cure, he was forgiven.

Had that been the only time Pasteur cheated the accepted rules, it would have been as mythic an event as it has seemed since. He was more than capable, however, of sidestepping rules and ethics, along with credit for his colleagues, in a more commonplace way. Pasteur can never be faulted for all the good he did. His process of killing off unwanted microorganisms in wine was applied later and most famously to milk. Without Pasteur, anthrax would be as mysterious a scourge as it was for millennia before he introduced a vaccine for it. The entire field of microbiology would have lagged by decades.

In the anthrax breakthrough, Pasteur relied on the work of a veterinary scientist, Jean Joseph Henri

Toussaint, in place of his own touted method for the oxidation that made the vaccine usable. He let everyone believe that he had used his own method, when he hadn't. In the aftermath of the tidal wave of good publicity that accompanied his demonstration, he worked on his own method until it finally worked. Then he slipped it into the process and revealed the whole method. Pasteur sometimes did things that were dangerous—such as telling the parents of the little boy who'd been bitten by the rabid dog that he had previously conducted a full course of experiments on his cure, using dogs. (I have to interject that I am an ardent anti-vivisectionist, but that doesn't change what Pasteur did.) In actual fact, which Pasteur kept secret at the time, he had experimented on only two or three dogs—and the results hadn't always been successful. In the aftermath, Pasteur concealed another small fact from all concerned, especially the reporters who had swarmed over his treatment of the boy, which required a series of shots over eleven days. The truth was that the boy never showed any symptoms of rabies and very possibly didn't have the disease. Pasteur's reports never examined that possibility. Gerald Geison, who analyzed Pasteur's private notebooks, which were themselves kept secret for almost a century, concluded that the monumental scientist was by nature deceitful. As another scientist wrote, "He would do anything to pull off a great public spectacle or win a prize." Descriptions like that one usher in cheating. The conundrum of Pasteur was that he was no less brilliant for being a cheater; it went along with his intensity in a gaping new field of study.

In the vein of rabies humor—of which there has never been much—King George II of Britain was struggling with the ineffective performance of his army in a campaign when a friend complained that the king's choice of a dogged new commander was *positively* mad. "Is he?" the king replied laconically. "I wish to my God he would bite some of my Generals, and make them mad, too." The same sort of proportional ethic might be applied to a heroic but somewhat cheating scientist such as Pasteur: the overall person might not be perfect. Would that society had ten more, though. In the realm of cheating, however, as well as research, finding even ten of that ilk through history wouldn't be easy, and the reason is a good one. If a leader in the field is known to be forgiven for sidestepping the rules, then what society will get next is not ten, but a thousand more cheaters with no heroism attached.

The question of who will cheat has itself been studied by scholars, and yes, the research has been fudged in many cases, but that should surprise no one who has read this far, so a sound and well-respected Columbia University report will be cited first. It was actually part of a series of volumes on character development among preteens. Among the findings of the four-year project was that "persons who attend the movies cheat most."

That seemed a harsh indictment, akin to charging ballet fans with compulsively hijacking oil tankers, but the study generally blamed emotion for interfering with self-control. The assumption was that people cheat when they lose control of themselves, a premise that doesn't fit someone like Itchy Novak, who cognitively and dispassionately desired to cheat. The authors of the study equated attraction to motion pictures with the capacity to be carried away, since movies of all kinds spark feelings, whether fear, joy, love, or seething anger that some boring movie ever got made in the first place. "Emotional children," concluded the report, "are more likely to be deceptive than others... Children who are well-mannered and are well treated by their parents are less deceptive than other children."

The Columbia researchers ultimately concluded that a child who is clean, well-behaved, predictable, intelligent, poised (unemotional), and comes from a good home is probably not going to cheat. At least not in comparison to what our study herewith might term, clinically, an actual child. After much thought, the only clean, well-behaved, predictable, intelligent, unemotional kid who comes to mind was in a Fredric March movie about a brainwashed Nazi youth. While actual children who boast even one of the listed characteristics are probably charming and will be a pleasure to bring to restaurants, the current study has not found them to be less likely to cheat than anyone else. Certainly not any less likely than the little bull in a china shop with dirty fingernails. The trouble for those Columbia sociologists is common to the entire guild of researchers into the field of cheating. Interviewees don't tell the truth. That is because when it comes to their own cheating, people barely know what the truth is.

About a generation ago, a long-distance runner was incensed at the advent of cheating in marathon races. The idea of plodding more than twenty-six miles on hard pavement has always struck me as a cruel thing to do to one's joints, not to mention one's innards, but nonetheless, the popularity of the long races surged in the 1980s. Cheaters soon followed. In pursuit of the glory without the concomitant sweat (and diarrhea), cheaters who started a race would either take a shortcut to the finish line or catch a ride, hopping back into the pack a few hundred yards before the finish line. A runner named Rosie Ruiz gained the most publicity in 1979–1980, when she was judged to have taken a subway for the majority of the New York City Marathon course. Even riding the subway, she only came in eleventh. I like to think that with the help of a subway, I could have done better than that. Apparently she thought the same thing, because by riding the T in Boston, she arranged to come in first in that city's marathon. After heated investigations, she was disqualified from both races. Ruiz was far from the only marathoner who was cheating, though. One poor man in Hawaii started a marathon there and then stopped for a large and leisurely breakfast with friends. Driving himself to a spot near the finish, he started running again and died instantly of a massive heart attack.

As a result of the many entrants jumping off and later back onto the course, organizers learned to track runners using computer and video technology. Cheaters then adopted a new means of racing without moving a muscle. They learned that one can hire some fit stringbean to run the course using one's own credentials, including the tracking device. In the Civil War, a person who hired someone to fight in his place was called a slacker. In marathons, the term is "braggart," because in no other way can a person eat eggs Benedict during the running of the race and still boast of a good finish. "Sure I finished," they will say that night at dinner, dropping a few barbecued spare ribs on top of their lasagna. "Look it up on the Internet if you don't believe me."

Before the 1980s, cross-country runners were a nerdy lot, a world unto themselves. Though it is hard to believe now, they actually got excited about sneakers before anybody else ever did. They thought that wearing just the right ones made a person cool. Can you imagine? They wore warm-up clothes—sweatshirts and lightweight sweatpants—*in public*. When marathons became all the rage, longtime runners had to grapple with the fact that they had been marathon before marathon was nifty. When confronted by the advent of cheating into their sport, they were absolutely aghast that anyone would actually avoid the chance to run twenty-six miles and 385 yards. And get rashes in intimate places or, for the men as well as the women, bloody nipples, all while running down a city street. Because they crave that very chance, they have always been outspoken against the cheaters. "I might fudge on my taxes," said one such runner, "or on my expense account, but I would never cut corners in a race."

That runner clearly stated why researchers fall short in their efforts to pinpoint a profile of the typical cheater. He reserved the right to be a cheater in some things and not others. By the peculiar laws of reverse identification found in this field, he is not a cheater in his own mind.

Ask a person if they cheat and they will typically list all the ways that they don't. They may never get around to owning up to the ways that they do.

While it is unseemly to question the perspective of my late colleagues in the Columbia paper, I nonetheless am going to surmise that when they questioned the many preteen subjects in their study, the clean-cut, well-poised, intelligent, and cool (unemotional) ones were more believable in denying deceit. It is also worth noting that such little people reflected the authors of the study, who happened to have had those same personal attributes. They trusted the kids who reminded them of themselves.

In conclusion, I distrust the conclusion that movie fans cheat. To the contrary, the only distinctive aspect of the movie fan's cluttered id is that it is more satisfying to sit still and watch *Dirty Rotten Scoundrels* three times in a row than to go through all the work and bother of actually cheating somebody.

A school psychologist named Harry Baker in Detroit used records of school incidents, rather than interviews, to pronounce that boys tended to be fighters and smart-alecks, but that "girls are worse than boys in lying, cheating and stealing. Cheating as a special trait occurred in 469 of the 1,357 cases. It is more common among older than younger pupils. Dull pupils cheat more than bright ones and the trait is closely related to arguing, interfering, lying and fighting."

Dr. Baker limited his pool of cheaters to those children who had been collared for the more conspicuous offenses, like kick-fighting, arguing, and interfering. His study missed a crucial pool of cheaters: the ones who got away with it. Itchy Novak, a Hall of Fame–caliber cheater, would never have been on any list of hotheads. Those 1,357 bad seeds, though, were the population of Dr. Baker's days in Detroit. Of course, he looked to them first.

The University of Wisconsin delivered a different message. They blamed mothers. "Cheaters," two professors there wrote, "appear to exhibit a set of behaviors similar to those produced by maternal overprotection. They seem to show a passive-dependent mode of adjustment, giving little of themselves in either intellectual endeavors or social relationships." (They should probably go to more movies.) In truth, the parental influence cannot be denied in some of the most serious cases. A study in New Jersey found a similar root cause of cheating: "It is pressure from the mother, rather than from the father," wrote the chief researcher, "that looms as the major factor in cheating behavior." My personal observation is that no one describes other people's mothers without actually describing their own; however, if the theses are expanded to parental influence from either side, then the two studies do explain a certain cheater, one of the rarest types, in fact. That is the person who is so attached to the opinion of the parent, even long after that parent is gone, that it becomes the sky in a very private universe. People who never see the rest of the world except as a satellite of their own universe can't perceive that they cheat. In times of conflict, it is obvious to them that the rest of the world is cheating.

An economist at Yale with a macroeconomic specialist's penchant for modeling tried to use an academic framework to quantify adultery. His paper sought to "explain the allocation of a spouse's time among spouse, paramour, and work." The impressively impenetrable formulas presented in the paper were based on data from surveys conducted by popular magazines.

The "coefficient estimates" in the Yale study indicated that the probability of adultery decreases with age. And yet, according to the coefficient estimates, it increases with the number of years that a spouse is stuck with the same old ball and chain. Specifically, the theory stated that "utility from affairs declines with age and that utility from marriage declines with length of marriage." This is the type of sentence that economics professors emit with bravura to an awestruck classroom. If a teacher ever said that over in the English department, however, where I was weaned, some freshman would raise their hand and ask in a surly voice how an adulterer can be young enough to be hot-blooded and concomitantly be married for a long, long, excruciatingly long time. A senior in the same class would write a short story with that plot and get an A plus. I know this from experience. It could be set on an island in the South Pacific.

Unless that's too Somerset Maugham. A Greek isle. Too much like *Fanny*. It could be set in Omaha.

A recent experiment departed from the various studies cited above. Rather than attempting to corral cheaters and then look them over, it sought to create cheaters. A scenario was designed by which participants had to assign a number of chores to others, one of the provisos being that they couldn't give themselves the easy job. In a purposeful glitch, the participants could easily realize that there was a way they could indeed give themselves the easy chore. There was absolutely no chance of anyone ever finding out—except, of course, the psychologists lined up on the other side of the one-way mirror. With consistency across an array of demographic groups, the experiment showed that the primary factor in whether or not a person will cheat is whether or not they think they will be caught. The apparent factors of neatness, religious observance, humility, education, charm, charity, reliability, and kindness to puppies are in no way connected to a refusal to cheat. Unfortunately, those characteristics offer a disguise for some of the most reprehensible of cheaters. A preliminary survey of embezzlers in my state over the past three years showed that they typically looked like frumpy grandmas or else models in the JCPenney catalogue. None was grizzled or wearing gaudy diamond jewelry. None was chomping a cigar or using a footlong cigarette holder. None was profane or even offbeat. None, to the best of my recollection, had an untucked shirt, a gaudy car, or a foreign accent—all sure signs, as everyone knows, of an embezzler. If the intended victim has it in mind that trustworthiness is connected to a particular type of person, then the deed is almost done. A good cheater becomes the type.

Another advantage of looking the part is that it feeds back into the cheater's own confidence that there is no chance of being caught.

Cheaters resist most of the standard demographic categories in part because they are usually born to the color of deceit in a single moment, as discussed in the previous chapter. The intersection of means, motive, and opportunity transforms other people into murderers. Cheaters are prone to an additional vector: confederacy. When others of one's peer group are

known to be cheating, the temptation to join them becomes almost irresistible. Employees playing hooky on
company time have the means to do so—quite easily
in many cases. A targeted study of department store
salesmen concluded that practically all of them faked
the employer out of work time. They considered that
they were underpaid and regarded cheating on time
as a way of evening the score. In that kind of environment, the pressure within the group is to cheat along
with the rest, or else appear to be on the side of the
employer. The confederacy of the others makes for another reason to turn one day. And on that day, to take
a four-hour lunch break.

"The best business in Juarez is cheating tourists," asserted a report on Mexico's fourth largest city in 1969.
In fact, according to the same report, a visit there was
more like a "shakedown" and practically everyone in
the city benefited, including the local officials who ex-
hibited "unbelievable indifference" at the "disastrous
state" of tourism in the border town. The report left a
picture of what confederacy as a factor in the decision
to cheat eventually becomes when it takes over completely: a replacement for the original rules.

The report on Juarez was memorable because it had
been issued by the head of the city's Chamber of
Tourism. The very next day, he retracted the whole
thing, all of it, and was never heard from again, at least
not publicly. Juarez's best business returned to normal.

In terms of motive, the inspiration may seem obvious: more of whatever it is that gives days their meaning, whether money, time, affairs—or victory. "I got
tired of losing," said a college basketball coach who

broke recruitment rules in order to entice better players. "It's as simple as that. I didn't want to get beat anymore." At first glance, that seems like a non-statement,
like saying that you like to breathe. Everybody wants
to breathe. Likewise, everybody wants to win, but that
doesn't mean that all people cheat.

Nobody particularly wants to pay taxes, either. When
one doesn't have the money, it is tough to pay up. But
when one is among the richest people in the country,
cheating on taxes is indicative of another type of thinking. Moses Annenberg, known as "Moe," had arrived
in America in about 1900, emigrating from Germany.
Starting in newspaper circulation wars, which could be
brutal, he earned a good salary and then built his own
business empire in publishing. He also earned money
through the flow of legitimate horse-racing information to illegitimate customers, mostly bookies around
the country. Annenberg cleared millions of dollars a
year at a time when a well-paid physician or executive
might make $10,000. In 1932, for example, his income
tax liability was $318,000. He wrote a check to the gov-
ernment for $308.

For Annenberg, $313,506 was equivalent to $308 for
most other people, so buying power wasn't the reason he cheated on his taxes. He did, however, increase
the size of his fortune by two and a half times in six
years, partially as a result of avoiding taxes equivalent to about 40 percent of his assets over that span.
For him, cheating became a challenge. He organized
eighty-four corporations "as devices to conceal a sub-
stantial part of his income," according to prosecutors.
Avoiding the IRS was a full-time sport for him.

According to a government official, his "desire to evade his income taxes was as keen as it was to make the income." Annenberg's defense during a subsequent trial on evasion charges was that his discrepancies were the result of sloppy bookkeeping, to which a prosecutor replied that by some rare coincidence, every instance of sloppiness left more money for Annenberg. The formerly penniless immigrant became a millionaire many times over, but it wasn't enough; the game was afoot and he had to chase it, through a maze of his own design. Eventually, he spent three years in prison and in addition gave the government $9 million in back taxes and penalties. Annenberg died a month after his release from jail; for those readers who may be worried, the family more than recouped its wealth later.

Opportunity, the last of four major conduits to cheating, may choose the person rather than the other way around. Not long ago, a young woman went to a concert by one of the renowned symphony orchestras in America. We will be discreet about which one. And we'll call the woman #77. That is not her real name.

A friend had bought two tickets, but they weren't near each other. Ms. #77 had a seat in the second row of the concert hall, off to the side: not the best seat in the house, in terms of acoustics and sightlines, but no one was sitting in front of her and it was fine.

#77 was listening to the music, as one does, and trying to find something at which to look. My own belief is that concert halls should put up pictures of innocuous seascapes and ducks on the horizon. Otherwise, the eyes can't help noting which French horn player has on cheap shoes, that all of the violin players have gained weight since they bought their concert clothes, and that the triangle player has yet to do a thing. The suspense becomes riveting and as it builds, one can't help wondering about the career path of a full-time triangle player. And still, not even one ting. Does it take years and years of study in Paris? One wonders whether they get paid the same as the pianist, who is actually sweaty. Very sweaty, as one takes note. An air conditioner would probably fit under the bench to—

The eyes of the average concertgoer drift thusly, while the music plays. But #77 couldn't help noticing that one of the cello players, a nice-looking middle-aged man, was looking at her. She naturally thought she was imagining it. He kept playing the music and because he didn't suddenly slip into "Turkey in the Straw," she had to think that his staring was just a way of concentrating. At some point, however, the fact was undeniable that the man was preternaturally obsessed with her—a total stranger. For #77, that point came that night in her apartment when she decided unequivocally that she had to go back for another concert. She obtained a seat that was close to the stage, but not on the same side as her previous outing. The music was rising and falling—we'll call it Opus 36 to conceal its identity—when #77 caught sight of the cello player. Immediately, his eyes sparkled with excitement, as he seemed unable to look away. Meanwhile, he kept playing and if he switched to "Hawaii Five-O," she wouldn't have noticed. When the concert was over, she didn't do anything. That is to say, she stayed in her seat.

The rest of the audience filed out. The ushers picked

up some of the trash left behind, the lights were dimmed, and #77 sat by herself. Eventually, just as she anticipated, the cello player walked out onto the stage and then skipped down the steps to greet her. Before either one knew it, they were leaving the concert hall together, holding hands, and #77 was probably wondering who would play her in the Hallmark Channel movie version of the romance, when in a matter-of-fact way, the cello player explained that he was married. He assured her that it didn't matter in any way and then he moved on in the conversation. The Hallmark movie was immediately canceled. Their relationship was not, however, and they embarked on a complicated affair, which was in retrospect mostly a waste of time for #77.

These things happen in a tattooed way at cowboy bars, but during Opus 36, it is quite another matter. And just possibly, it could have been the real thing. That opportunity had been more than one particular nice woman could ignore.

CHAPTER 9

Power Play

When cheaters prosper

Yeah sex is cool and all but have you ever found your entire final on quizlet."

To translate that tweet into a different language, one called grammar, which wastes untold milliseconds every single day for those fluent in it:

Yeah, sex is cool and all, but have you ever found your entire final on Quizlet?

Quizlet is an app that peppers users with scholastic-type questions, such that they can measure their grasp of required course material. That much harkens to flash cards and practice tests, which have been in use for a long time. As the app has developed, though, actual exams have often been posted and then ferreted out by students who have no compunction about using them.

The tweet above was written in 2018 by a college student in the spring semester of her freshman year at a university in the South. It received 253 "likes" and 58 "retweets," which doesn't seem nearly enough for the import of her message.

"Yeah sex is cool and all but have you ever found your entire final on quizlet."

Colleges in this country started out in the 1600s with the overriding mission to turn out ministers. By the 1700s, they were also turning out mathematicians, doctors, and candidates for the bar. By the 1800s, so many other subjects were included that colleges made a strength of the liberal arts. By the 1900s, technology, which was purposefully specialized, competed with the liberal arts, which were just as purposefully broad in scope. All of those strains can still be found on campuses, but the 2000s have broken with the concept that bound those centuries of academic life into a continuum: the concept of what college is. For that reason, cheating has found a comfortable place, a place where it has become cool and all that.

Over the past few decades, the student body at large has transformed college life, even while students as individuals wend their way to the finish line. They may not know much—to wit, a large proportion, according to a recent poll, can't say what two sides fought in the Civil War...the American Civil War. But they know exactly what college is for and what they want from it.

The Graduate School of Education at the University of California at Los Angeles studies the subject of students. The Cooperative Institutional Research Program (CIRP), which is based there, conducted its first research project in 1966 by polling 254,480 incoming freshmen at 307 colleges across the country. Hundreds of questions were included then and still are, in what has become an annual project. Many of the responses barely budge across the years, leading to the triumphant impression that college kids are just like their grandparents. By looking at the section in the CIRP reports labeled "Objectives Considered to be 'Essential' or 'Very Important,'" however, one can peer into the expectations of the new collegians, expectations that reveal the modern answer to the question of what college is. One response in particular, supported by others, kicks a hole in the picture of college life as it was drawn in all the previous centuries. That response has changed college, as well as the instinct to cheat one's way through it.

For those now swiping through pages on Quizlet to see what that one response is, I have thoughtfully provided cribbing in advance by putting it in bold print. Hint: it's on the fourth line of the chart:

FIG. 9.1—Lifetime Objectives: The Percentage of College Freshmen
Who Considered Each One "Essential" or "Very Important,"
According to Annual CIRP Surveys

The five objectives selected (out of twelve to twenty in the surveys) indicate major motivating interests of America's freshmen. In alternating decades, two years have been included to reduce the chance of an anomaly skewing the analysis.

Objectives Considered to Be "Essential" or "Very Important"	1967	1973	1976	1986	1992	1996	2006	2014	2016
Achieve in a performing art	11.3	23.9	10.2	10.5	10.5	12.2	15.7	16.7	17.5
Be an authority in my field	67.8	57.6	73.5	71.8	68.5	64.1	58.2	60.2	58.7
Develop a philosophy of life	82.9	73.7	57.7	40.6	45.6	42.1	46.3	44.6	46.8
Be very well off financially	**43.5**	**45.5**	**61**	**73.2**	**73**	**74.1**	**73.4**	**82.4**	**82.3**
Raise a family	NA	58.2	57.5	67	70.6	72.2	75.5	72.3	71.7

"Achieve in a performing art" has never garnered a high percentage. Except of course during the *if-Slade-can-sell-millions-of-records-then-who-can't* bounce in 1973. The twenty-first-century mini-surge probably relates to the advent of media venues such as reality TV and YouTube channels, which constitute performing arts in some new sense.

Two responses measure seriousness of purpose in a more intellectual sense. The first, "Be an authority in my field," indicates a sincere passion for learning. The next, "Develop a philosophy of life," displays a contemplative type of mind embracing a deep challenge. Both of those percentages have dropped like stones. From 1967 to 2016, "Be an authority" fell from 67.8 to 58.7. "Develop a philosophy" fared even worse, being essential to 82.9 percent of freshmen in 1967 and just 46.8 in 2016.

The remaining two objectives relate entirely to life after college. According to the framework of each of them, college is not an open-ended process, as in the previous two, but quite the opposite: a means to a predetermined end. "Raise a family" is part of that picture. Obviously, there is nothing unusual about wanting to raise a family, except that students seventeen or eighteen years old have become more locked into that objective than were their predecessors over the last fifty years. The real key to the twenty-first-century college student, however, is the desire to be very well off financially. That objective was in the bottom third of the responses (by percentage) in the early years of the survey. In the new century, it easily ranked first. The vast majority of college kids—more than four-fifths—mainly want to be very rich. The effect that their predilection has on college falls into two major categories, and one minor one.

For most of those four-fifths, the drive to be very rich turns college into vocational school. It is a place to learn a trade, preferably one high on the spectrum. According to the philosophy, such as it is, of life that they have developed, they don't *care* what the sides were in the Civil War, because they don't need to dig down deep and utter "North" and then "South" in order to get a job (unless they happen to be majoring in tour-guiding, with a Bull Run minor). That which is irrelevant to the job is unneeded.

In a smaller sector of that four-fifths, to the contrary, nothing that can be learned in college is applicable to the intention to be rich. The diploma is all that counts, opening, as it does, doors, and conveying, as it will, respectability. Itchy Novak, who was cited in Chapter 8, represented that perspective. John D. Rockefeller, who also had an early desire to be well-off financially, never went to college. He came of age in the 1850s, when few people interested in business sought a baccalaureate degree. Rockefeller's contention was that in his day, the greatest asset any businessperson possessed was a sterling reputation. Only with that would come jobs and orders, credit, trust, and opportunities. And with those things came fortunes, large, small, or epic. From Rockefeller's point of view, as of 1926:

> There is no mystery in business success. The great industrial leaders have told time and again the plain and obvious fact that there can be no per-

manent success without fair dealing that leads to widespread confidence in the man himself, and that is the real capital we all prize and work for.

Full disclosure: some people consider John Rocke-feller to have been a flagrantly unfair dealer, as well as a cheater and a crook.

Fuller disclosure: I don't. His quote is not included to introduce that discussion, however, but to prove that until long into the twentieth century, reputation was highly personal property in the world of getting very rich. One's family might give that reputation a good launch, but it still remained an individual's very own "real capital," as Rockefeller put it. Eventually, the twentieth century developed an invention to replace or materially augment that understanding: a degree in business administration. By way of an undergradu-ate concentration or the even more burnished master's (MBA), "reputation" was packaged and purveyed and all but guaranteed to be puncture-proof. Reputation in the current sense doesn't need to be built over time, not when it is so sturdily prefabricated. Students who earnestly want knowledge in management and related skills pursue such degrees. So do those who just need a diploma that will slide them along on the chosen path to jobs and orders, credit, trust, and opportuni-ties. College students who look upon a degree as an inconvenient necessity comprise a small but relentless proportion of the four-fifths in question.

The two types of students described above comprise the majority of those who have changed what college is: those whose prime objective is to be very well off financially. There is another type of money-mad student with pathetically shallow goals. I speak from some experience, being the only senior in my high school yearbook to list their prime objective in life as owning a Rolls-Royce. Where others desired a career in medicine or the chance to "help children all over the world," I also specified that I wanted a large estate in England. I've since matured, of course, all the way to wanting a Bentley and a large estate in France, but I feel certain that I'd have checked "being very well off financially" as an objective when I was a freshman in college. I may even have checked it twice for emphasis. The only codicil is that a relative of mine professed that the easiest way to make money is to really love your work. For that reason, college wasn't a time to think about jobs, but to follow the usual academic path, varied as it was. For the purposes of this study, the example of one person proves the existence of a third type within the four-fifths: students who regard college in the traditional sense of liberal arts, but who harbor drastically expensive objectives to boot. And who admire John Rockefeller.

The two major types of students described previously, the ones who are in college to prepare for a specific job or to gain a valuable diploma, are inclined in varying degrees to believe that college is an encapsulated experience, a self-contained section of their lives. Cheating in those circumstances is equally encapsulated, under the belt-buckle ethic: *git 'er done*.

Not all students in the four-fifths cheat, but the point is that they can do so and still achieve their expressed objective. They can cheat a little or a lot in college and then hop over the rubble into the real world of becoming very well off financially. That possibility is practically nonexistent if one is trying to become an authority in a chosen field. It is outright impossible when developing a life philosophy. The difference that these factors have made lies in reconfiguring what college is. What was once the beginning for students exposed there to a more enlightened way of thinking has become more simply the end of the educational portion of life. Each attitude is valid. No doubt a veritable parade of my college classmates who were interested in the diploma, not the details, are at this very minute driving in their Bentleys to the Large Estate Owners Club of France. While I sit here, typing.

That's all right.

The prevalent view of college, though, has caused cheating to reverberate through other circles of American society. The most disturbing involve the seismic shift whereby parents lead, follow, or get out of the way of their child's cheating. They fall along a range that includes (1) failing to punish their children for cheating, (2) seeing nothing wrong with cheating, (3) defending it, (4) cooperating with it, or (5) spearheading it. The old cat-and-mouse game underlying school cheating gave great satisfaction to non-cheaters, who would taunt or mutter, depending on their age, "You're going to get in big trouble..." Even if the cheater never did get caught, the smudge of secret shame hung overhead. One can look at a person who is long into adulthood and think, "If I ever told your mother what you did in Calculus 244, you'd fry." In the case of complicit parents, though, the cat has become just another mouse.

The evidence is that parental complicity is a twenty-first-century phenomenon, though it had antecedents in earlier times. One common instance lay with students who broke honor codes, especially at the service academies, by not reporting any whiff of cheating about which they heard. For that infraction, they received exactly the same punishment as the cheaters, except at the Naval Academy, which is slightly more lenient. In major cheating scandals at West Point (1951, 1976), Annapolis (1992), and the Air Force Academy (1965), parents complained bitterly about their children being ruined when they absolutely didn't cheat but did hold true to the military's blood loyalty within the ranks. "My boy didn't cheat—he just refused to be a stool pigeon," said Roy Entyre, whose son was forced out of the Air Force Academy in the 1965 affair, which involved a stolen test that made the rounds in the dormitories. "We sent our boy to the academy with honor and integrity—what have they done to him?" said a mother in the same position at the time.

The disappointment of the non-cheating cheater, someone who has just been done in by an honor code, is understandably acute. But out of earshot of the parents, one might concur with the Santa Fe man who railed that, "We, the citizens, should thank God the cheaters were discovered before they had a chance to sell defense secrets to the enemy—or refuse to 'snitch' on those who did."

In this century, much has changed. The grumbling of a sympathetic mother or father has grown into the rapacity of an *agent provocateur* who intends that their kid will get ahead. Their kid *will* get ahead.

"Here's my excuse," wrote Lisa Miller in *New York* magazine in 2013, explaining the fact that "while the kiddie race to the top among the most competitive people may elicit the most grotesque behaviors, the fact is that all kinds of parents seize the advantage for their kids." Her excuse for any such inclinations was modern: "The future is uncertain, and no one knows what skills kids will need to get by in war or warming or economic collapse. The accoutrements of middle-class stability and comfort feel like they're slipping away, even to those of us living smack in the middle of them." That is one theory. Previous generations, however, which lived through regular spasms of war and economic collapse, as well as environmental catastrophes such as floods and storms, droughts and conflagrations, didn't insist that the end of the world would be all better, as long as the firstborn got into Dartmouth. Miller was correct, though, in pointing out that the kiddie race is becoming crowded with adults.

In late fall of 2001, the dividing line was crossed when a biology teacher in the small town of Piper, Kansas, assigned her tenth-grade students to collect leaves from local trees and then describe them in botanical terms. Her 118 students had not only learned in the class to tell a petiole from a stipule, they also had been specifically admonished against plagiarism. Twenty-eight of them didn't get either lesson. When they handed in leaf descriptions that had been lifted from other sources, the teacher, Ms. Pelton, gave them zeros, which effectively left them with a failing grade in the course. The high school principal looked the matter over and concurred with her decision. Many of the parents did not agree, however, and they bypassed the teacher and the principal, taking their ire to the members of the school board. They filled a board meeting, claiming that the teacher was too inexperienced to judge the kids, that the students couldn't be expected to know that copying was the same as plagiarism, and that the harsh penalty would affect the students' whole future and chance of getting into the college of their choice. One imagines that there was little that the incensed parents didn't say in ongoing private meetings with the board members. At a meeting on December 11, the board voted unanimously to overrule Ms. Pelton. It ordered her to pass all but one of the cheating students.

Over the course of the next few months, Pelton quit, some of the board members were replaced, the county district attorney descended on the town to file charges, and the principal submitted his resignation in protest. Everything had changed in Piper except the proud parents of the students who cheated. In another vote, five months after the first, the newly chagrined school board looked at the issue again. Once again it voted unanimously that the teacher was in the wrong; the high school was ordered to give the cheaters passing grades.

Chapter 3 described the compulsion to cheat individuals specifically because of their demographics (ethnicity, gender, etc.). Some members of the general public, however, distort the playing field for the exact opposite reason. They are prejudiced in *favor* of certain groups.

In the wake of a 1965 cheating scandal involving tournament bridge, an editorialist for an American paper exclaimed that the incident was "all the more amazing because the alleged cheaters are British."

The British were something of an obsession with Americans in the 1960s, what with the originality of their music, clothing, humor, plays, and cars, all of that color emerging out of the gentle permanence of their way of life. At the same time, American culture was more artificial than ever before or since, with a way of life celebrating the disposable. The fad for Swinging London was even more irresistible because it was perched on three or four hundred years of the British sometimes proving but always announcing their belief in fair play. For those reasons, Americans could hardly believe their ears when a pair of Brits were accused of cheating in bridge at its highest level. "This is upsetting to our image of British honor and probity," wrote the newspaper editors. "Maybe we are just naïve to expect that the villains in a case like this would be from Ruritania or Reno." But not Puddleby-on-the-Marsh.

Terence Reese, a famed author of bridge books, and Boris Schapiro, a well-known cardplayer in London, were competing against a pair of Americans in the World Bridge Championships in Argentina. One of the Americans noticed that Reese was holding his hand in an odd way. Looking to the other side of the table, he realized that Schapiro was doing the same. He told his partner later on and they took mental notes then and written ones on a day when Reese and Schapiro were playing against an Italian duo. A clear picture soon emerged.

The dominant part of bridge is communicating the strength of one's hand to one's partner, using the bidding process. It isn't simple. If you have three good, strong diamonds, the last thing you will bid, in most systems, is "Four diamonds!!! Oh boy, oh boy, oh boy!" Because you want your partner, not the opposition, to know what you have, you are more likely in that case to bid two spades. According to your carefully preconceived bidding strategy, your partner will then think, "Aha. Two spades. My partner has strong diamonds and oh look, I have four of them myself." On that certainty, your partner will then bid one club. And you'll know.

Bridge bidding is incomprehensible to those with a literal mind. For that reason, such people prefer Whac-A-Mole. You see the thing, you hit the thing. Bridge bidding, however, is all consuming to those who would rather hold hundreds of possibilities in mind than have a padded hammer in hand. Reese would focus so fiercely on the bidding that Schapiro once bet a mutual friend that a naked woman could walk by the table and Reese wouldn't break his concentration. The experiment was duly performed and Reese glanced blankly at her, his eyes holding tight to the complexity of that moment in the game.

In Argentina, the American team compared their detailed notes on the ways that Reese and Schapiro held their cards, using left hands most of the time. Occasionally the right. The setup was rarely repeated, as the player might have one finger showing on the back of the fan made by a "hand," or two, three, or four fingers there. The fingers might be spread out or pressed together.

Reese and Schapiro, it bears repeating, were among the half-dozen best bridge players in the world, possessing in their mammoth intellects data applicable to any situation, able to provide razor-sharp analysis in a flash, even or especially in the heat of competition. And yet, Reese and Schapiro were playing tournament bridge in a style that would make perfect sense to a Whac-A-Mole player. While that thought would be disgusting to either one of them, it is reasonable to a less ceremonious type of intellect that if you want to tell your partner that you have three hearts, *why not* hold the cards with three fingers showing? That was the basis of the Reese/Schapiro scheme. The number was generally doubled if the fingers were spread out. When there were no hearts at all, Schapiro and Reese used their right hands. "The hypothesis was checked against 17 deals," wrote an American bridge correspondent, "and the numbers of fingers corresponded with the number of hearts in every case."

The captain of the British team immediately withdrew the two champion players from the tournament, contending that Schapiro had confessed. Both players, however, publicly denied cheating in the maelstrom that followed. "I had no difficulty," Reese later wrote, "in maintaining my point that there were many simpler, more undetectable and equally clear ways of communicating." He further insisted that "information about heart length [quantity] was less valuable than about certain other features, my point having been that a winning advantage could easily be established in a less elaborate way." Bemused astonishment is a common response to charges of cheating among the powerful:

"*Do you really think that I'd go to all the trouble*...to com-municate by fingers about hearts, when I could have communicated by eyelashes about spades?*"

Yes.

The contention of Reese, who was more vociferous than Schapiro, was that whatever happened, the play had not been affected. In bridge, every detail of a game is recorded and so he and other experts pointed to the fact that they had done nothing that could be traced to an illicit knowledge of the "length" of their hearts. In respect to cheating, however, that is an entirely moot point. As in any act of betrayal, cheating is judged by those who have been cheated. Reese cannot decide whether his unfair advantage was neutralized by his de-cision not to profit from it. The judges and, most of all, his opponents were the only ones in a position to see his activities for what they were.

Because the British Bridge League ultimately came to no conclusion about the culpability of its two stars, both Schapiro and Reese continued to enjoy the status of esteemed authorities to the end of their lives. Decades after the scandal, though, something new was added to the case. After Reese died, one of his col-leagues announced that he had been authorized to tell the truth about the incident, but only after forty years had passed and both of the participants were dead. In 2005, he duly explained that Reese "confided that in the 1960s he had been planning to write a highly re-searched, in-depth book on cheating at cards and other indoor games and activities, commenting that cheats should be pilloried and their methods exposed...He persuaded a reluctant Schapiro that, as world champions, it would be quite unthinkable that they would cheat, that no one would be even paying attention to such an idea, and that in any event, absolutely no signaled information would be used in any way whatsoever during the actual play."

The argument Reese drew through the years was as follows: he hadn't cheated in Argentina (his fingers just went a certain way when he held the cards), but if he did cheat, he didn't use the information gleaned, so it wasn't cheating, but if it was cheating, it was for a book to be written on cheating, so it wasn't cheating. It was anti-cheating! He was, by God, a hero.*

The strategy Reese used to evade the charges was simply to grope along with whatever needed to be said or done until he could find enough gray area for himself. That would leave the ninety books he had published, mostly on bridge, plenty of room in the sun. As long as he was in the gray, defenders stepped forward to counter his detractors. In time, the scandal became a cottage industry, always ripe for a column or a new book or even dramatization in various media. By his own design, Reese watched as his own

---

*   **n.b.** As a person who actually makes a living writing about cheating, I'd like to counter Reese's claim that he was only doing research in Argentina. Even we who are in the profession full-time don't proffer that excuse. We have high standards, most of the time. When I told my editor that I planned to go on the DarkNet and obtain by scurrilous methods an authentic degree (not merely a diploma) from Yale University, all in the name of research, he said the following: "Don't do that! I definitely don't want you to ruin your life for this book." I am not sure which part of the plan worried him—that I'd cheat or that I'd become a Yalie—but Reese's editor, no doubt, would have said much the same thing to him. One tests out the cheating arts at the dining table against one's relatives, not at the world championships.

profile became even grayer, that being the color of life for a cheater.

In response to Reese's argument: If his signaling was really for a book on cheating, he would have behaved like any *true* author on cheating or anything else and taken advantage of a million dollars' worth of free publicity, publishing the thing even before his plane landed from Buenos Aires, but since he never did get around to writing that ninety-first book, the one on cheating at cards, it's obvious that the only thing he did on the plane from Buenos Aires was sort through a ragged list of pathetic excuses and choose the book-research one. If he were, however, researching a book on cheating and it were published, it would've been shelved in the juvenile section, because the style of cheating he and Schapiro invented was so on the nose, it could have been detected at the Go Fish World Championships, let alone the bridge event. Frankly one would think that any bona fide intellectual giants from the nation of Alan Turing and Bletchley Park would have added a code to their digits (i.e., the number of hearts in one's hand will be equal to the number of fingers showing multiplied by *pi* and divided by *m*, where *m* is equal to the number of cigarettes in the ashtray). They were lousy cheaters, in addition to being lousy cheaters.

That didn't stop them, however, from emerging with their influence intact, their prestige and power still unmatched in the world of bridge.

CHAPTER 10

Rooked but Good

Cheating against cheaters

When the right chance comes along, nothing else matters, least of all the future. The present is the good part of life. All in all, the future is nothing more than the possibility of getting beat up. "I had about three dollars in my pocket," a hustler named Joe said of his invitation to play in a high-stakes euchre game in upstate New York. "We set the stakes at $100 a game; $10 a box, $1 a point." In other words, if his luck was average, he had enough for about a quarter of a hand. Joe's opponent was the biggest gambler in the city, a restaurateur who, as another acquaintance related, "spent money as though it were going out of style, although even after casually winning or losing $30,000 without batting an eye, he would go to his restaurant and count the oyster crackers to make sure he wasn't getting clipped."

For Joe, the chance to play a big-time player didn't come around often. Buying in with only three dollars was an invitation to trouble, but he couldn't resist. Adding to the aura of destiny was that fact that the restaurateur was half drunk. As Joe took on Goliath, people stood around the table watching. "I am cheating the guy real good," Joe recalled. "He is sort of fumbling around with his cards and I am in cahoots not only with MY partner but with his partner, too, which is pretty good odds, having three guys out of four in the game on the same side. I am winning $5,000 cash money, paid after every game, when the telephone rings."

The restaurateur was called to the phone. When the conversation was over, he put the phone down and returned to his seat.

"What was that call?" one of the onlookers asked.

"Oh, a guy who was watching us play went next door and called to tell me that Joe is cheating me." The room fell silent. All eyes were on the restaurant man. "I told him, 'So what? I know he is cheating me, but this is the only game in town tonight.'"

The euchre game continued, much as before. "And do you know," Joe recalled, "that son-of-a-gun wound up beating me for the entire $5,000—plus my three bucks. I think he cheated, the dirty rat!"

A cheater's greatest fear is not getting caught. It is getting cheated, which is to say: dominated on his own terms. When a crook like Joe is left startled and reaching out for rules, he is ruined, because the naked truth is that no one depends more on the standing covenant than a cheater. It is that understanding upon which he or she builds, either to rook the guileless or to give a dual life its screen. A cheater who has been cheated can no longer reconcile his place in the world, what makes him special. He's no longer on the outside of a good world. He's smack in the middle of his own world and a loser in it.

The restaurateur might have had the whole game planned, even down to his friend telephoning at the right time, so that he could make sure the other three were wide awake when he got busy draining their bankrolls. On an off night in Rochester, he nabbed Joe's three dollars, and perhaps more important, he had the most fun a person could have without a storage bin of oyster crackers. The person who cheats a cheater counts on the secondary payoff. None of it may seem worth the angst to those looking at the situation from the outside, but in the mind of the cheater, that balance rests on a different fulcrum. A woman who has an extramarital affair feels, typically, as though she found something that had been missing from her life. That's the basic motivation. One step further, and looking for a secondary payoff, the woman who starts an affair specifically because her husband has previously betrayed her feels triumphant. But she isn't.

"My dear husband," wrote just such a woman in a letter, "I am not leaving you, but I am cheating every chance I get and it is keeping me sane. Last year I met a man who made me come alive after I was sure I had died inside. The romance went out of our marriage long ago. It has been years since we had a real conversation. You are either too busy or too tired to talk. You made me feel like a drag, a bore, a nuisance and finally, a nothing. When I found lipstick on your shirts I was supposed to believe it was red marking crayon. You refused to go to church with me because you said you could worship God better on the golf course than with a bunch of hypocrites."

Far be it for me to defend a man who was either necking with another woman or engaging in a highly unusual relationship with a red marking crayon; however, he does have a point about the hypocrites in his wife's church, inasmuch as she can scorn him and then celebrate herself for the same extramarital activity.

Far be it, too, for me to pick on anyone, such as this wife, who was ever made to feel like a nothing. However, she wrote the letter in part to mark her victory: she'd cheated the cheater. It's best that, as she later noted, she never sent it. Reflex cheating only works in complicated schemes in certain fields, but never in romance. "Never" is a big word, but it neatly covers the effort to even the score. In the race to betray, the person who follows suit can never take the lead. It's too late.

One of the most stiletto cases of cheating a cheater was perpetrated by a Missouri man named Ed Bryson, who made major advances in credit-card fraud. He veritably dallied with the issuing banks, boasting, "I knew their operation so well that they knew they couldn't stop me." Bryson roamed back and forth between St. Louis, Missouri, and the Illinois region of East St. Louis. He noticed that many people, after making a purchase with a credit card, would toss the receipt in the nearest receptacle. After Bryson snatched such a receipt, he'd go home and send a check to pay for the item, while also requesting in a note that the company change the billing address to his own and also send a new card. Up to that point, his game was identity theft, a type that was especially hard to catch, since customer complaints about bills being mysteriously paid in full are so rare. Bryson would be stealthy at first, buying and duly paying for a series of small items with each fake card. Building a bit of credit, he then bought a truckload of big-ticket items that could be sold for cash. The scheme went on for seven years, during which time he developed a typically ruinous drug habit. Whether one abhors his success or envies it, it is depressing that he threw the money away on drugs.

According to Bryson, the four biggest credit-card companies were aware of his extensive cheating and finally came to the conclusion that they had to act. "They asked me to stop defrauding them and each company would pay me," Bryson said in testimony before the Illinois Legislative Commission. "I knew their operation so well that they knew they couldn't stop me and I guess they figured the salary would be less than I would steal from them."

Honest people everywhere can pause for a moment here X to wonder where they went wrong in life.

Most credit-card customers only get form letters from their banks, coldly friendly notes describing how groovy life is going to be with a new array of fees. Such customers might well wonder how the cartel of credit-card companies conveyed their offer to Mr. Bryson. Did they write him a personal letter at home? "Dear Mr. Bryson, we know who you are, where you live, and that you have been cheating us out of a fortune. We have therefore decided that we want to give you a ton of money." Did they place a personal ad in the *East St.*

Louis Monitor? "PARTY ROOKING US: Pls reply soon-est, wish to pay same ton money." Did they send a note to one of his aliases? "Dear Mrs. Loghisanml, How are you, dear? Will you kindly ask Mr. Bryson to stop into the bank sometime this week? Any day will be fine. On behalf of the entire credit-card department, I wish to present to him three dimes of Detroit Pink and score him a deck of woolahs."

However it was communicated, Bryson turned down the offer of a salary, continuing his activities as before. In the course of his scheme, his last step with each fraudulent card was the cleverest of all. It also illus-trates the spirit of annihilation that lurks at the core each time a cheater cheats a cheater. After using a credit card for exactly two months, Bryson was savvy enough to retire it. He didn't dispose of it in another state, however, nor did he chop it into pieces, throw it into an incinerator, or all three for good measure. Instead, whenever he was finished with a card, he'd drop it on the floor of a bus station or somewhere else where impecunious people tend to pass. "I was hop-ing whoever found the cards would use them," Bryson explained, "and get caught the first time. In this way they would get the rap for all the other purchases I had made and it covered my tracks."

Eliciting sympathy for the kind of person who finds a credit card and immediately uses it might have been thought impossible—until Edmund Bryson came along. First, then, we must set aside the image of the person at the bus station who thought their ship came in, because they could treat themselves to a couple of Mallo Cups and a Slim Jim. And we must set aside the next image, too, as that person rots away in jail for all of the hundreds of refrigerators, lawn tractors, TV sets, and power tools that Bryson bought, sold, and then shoved up his nose or into his veins. Instead, the focus is on Bryson. In terms of cheating strategy, he found a way to remain in the shadows, while pushing someone else into the glare.

Bryson was eventually arrested on drug offenses, which would not have happened if he had spent all his money more wisely. He hadn't killed the goose that laid the golden eggs, exactly, but he had taken her for granted.

A similar scheme, one that was even more spiteful, if that is possible, was perpetrated by a college professor. It was also delightful. The frustration felt by professors has been going on for a long time: dedicating one's life to teaching, nurturing young minds, and inspiring them to a lifetime of learning, only to discover that the little turds weren't interested in even a week of learning, but instead went out and bought the final papers that they submitted as their own. According to one study, nearly all college students have cheated. While that is hard to believe, the far more frightening corollary is that some large proportion of students don't consider cheating as anything except a practical means to a virtuous end. "It's a dog-eat-dog thing," said a student who was in her junior year at a college near Phoenix, Arizona. "If no one cheated, I wouldn't cheat either. My parents would really like me to get good grades.

"And as I go into teaching," she continued, "I'll be put at the head of the list if I have good grades." The broader image of a student cheating her way into a teaching career is too much like a serpent eating its tail to dwell upon. To the Phoenix student, though, it was a rather unremarkable part of the process. She was as matter-of-fact as the mother at a parent-teacher conference who recalled her family's annoyance with the local high school when she was growing up. She had received an A for a paper that she wrote for her English class. A few years later, when her brother handed in the same paper to his English teacher, he only got a C. The family took it as proof that teachers are crooked.

People who look at a school and see only a diploma helped turn the sale of compositions into big business during the 1970s. Corporations arose on the supply side and brazenly advertised in college newspapers. Termpapers Unlimited, Inc. in Boston was almost as good as its name, selling ten thousand term papers during its first semester in operation. A competitor, Termpaper, Inc., in the San Francisco area, also thrived, advertising to not only sell papers, but to also purchase them: "We'll buy your essays, themes, theses, term papers, dissertations." Some college professors were outraged and no doubt made notes on a syllabus for a 300-level course: "AMERICANISM, IMPERIAL-ISM, and CAPITALISM IN ESOTERISM'S CANNI-BALISM: New Perspectives." Other teachers—many others—burned the midnight oil and wrote papers to sell to the companies. They either sent them on a wholesale basis (and in a case of double-layered cheating, did so by skimming off the best papers submitted in class each semester) or they were hired to write papers on specific topics.

So it was that one of the most upstanding professors at a Maryland college, a member of the English literature faculty, adopted the brand of "cheater" and sold term papers to a "paper mill." After all, one could make as much money writing papers on the side as teaching in a major university. In some respects, such professors are innocent of actual cheating. They compose an essay that may take the form of a term paper, but they don't direct what should be done with that essay. For all they know, a customer may simply buy it, read it, and enjoy it. Professors who sell papers might use just such a non-offender defense; they, however, did at some point accept the covenant of honest scholarship, which any market for term papers serves to undermine.

One of the papers that the English professor in Maryland sold very astutely presented a study of Shakespeare's *Romeo and Juliet*, focusing on the character of Banquo. The professor's closest friends were dismayed. One of them, however, Dr. Patricia Marby Harrison, soon realized that her colleague's cottage industry was actually a form of what she termed "guerrilla warfare," noting that the prof "included just enough errors that a teacher would be alerted." And the student would flunk, because Banquo was a character in *Macbeth*.

I hope you knew that.

When a Bergen County, New Jersey, man by the name of Randy made the decision to become a lawyer, he considered two choices to attain that goal. He could go to law school for three years. Or he could talk to a guy he knew.

The guy, whose street name was Sam, ran a good business, one might even say a brilliant one. He

charged people $1,000 for a law license, promising to
save them three years, as well as a summer of study
for the bar exam. He could have charged the same
amount for a medical license, a pilot's or an engineer's
license, but then he would have been in trouble, because he didn't know how to get any of those things.
Dissatisfied customers then would have gone to the police. He didn't know how to get a blank law license,
either, but the very basis of his business was that no
one would go to the district attorney and admit to trying to get a fake law license. How would one even start
that conversation? The scheme was a thing of beauty
and a public service, too, inasmuch as it kept innumer-
able dunderheads from practicing law in New Jersey.
In terms of this study, Sam illustrates the stranglehold
that a cheater in one sphere—fraud—can deliver to a
cheater in a very different activity—impersonation. He
didn't, however, count on someone like Randy.

When Randy realized that no license was forthcom-
ing, he naturally wanted his $1,000 back. Nonetheless,
he should have accepted the fact that according to the
dictates of cheating, he had been rendered inert. He
was lying on the ground, as it were, flat as a board,
and Sam was still moving fast. Did Joe in Rochester
demand his three dollars from the restaurateur? No,
of course not. Even after flopping as a cheat, however,
Randy displayed a lack of character. Rather than accept
his fate, he fled the gray area in a panic and scampered
back to all that he had rejected when he first sought to
sidestep the legal system and those who devote their
lives to it. Randy went to the district attorney.

After no doubt walking around the DA's office to

look at the law license framed there—and to make sure the signature at the bottom wasn't Sam's—Randy pressed charges. He actually crossed the line. Sam was immediately arrested for obtaining money under false pretenses, a felony known in the New Jersey statutes as "theft by deception."

Randy testified at the trial, showing what a rare orator the profession had lost, as he exclaimed, "He's a crook! He took my money knowing he could get to Mars faster than he could get me a license to practice law." Randy was absolutely right in every respect, even the interplanetary, yet the judge quickly dismissed the charges, on the basis that the law was intended to protect innocent victims "and not people who claim they have been cheated by their co-conspirators."

The case might have been appealed on the humble suggestion that the law is intended to protect everyone, not merely the lily-pure. For the sake of that argument, we can raise the stakes to the most serious felony of them all; the courts would surely convict a murderer who shot a victim in cold blood, even if the victim had just murdered someone—who had murdered yet another person the day before that. Those infractions don't cancel out, but cheating ones usually do, on the rare occasions when they go to law. Instead of Sam going free, he and Randy both should have been in jail. The legal world, however, was as uncomfortable with them as they finally became with it. Sam went free. Randy just went.

CHAPTER 11

Game Change

Will a cheater ever stop cheating?

Throughout most millennia, people were too busy avoiding sudden death themselves to worry about which sports teams made the playoffs. In those long years, a good season meant food. "Track" meant food and "field" meant food. Rooting, of course, meant a carrot. Prehistoric peoples didn't waste words on sports, let alone billions of their hard-earned dollars.

Skipping over ancient times, when amphitheaters teemed with fans of blood sport, a survey of athletic events lands on the gaggles of spectators in more recent centuries who watched local athletes play games on the village green. It was in the late 1700s that horse racing and boxing led the way into professional sports, producing stars known far and wide. Those sports then veered into the even longer history of cheating, as professionals were readily presumed to fix outcomes. Rich people tugged on the ethics from the other direction by encouraging amateurism. The assumption was that while an amateur *might* cheat, a professional did so as a matter of course. Not every time or all the time, but the possibility was in the air. A professional would weigh the factors.

Townball was one of the sports seen on the village greens, having been played by either that name or the more modern "baseball" for at least five hundred years. It is apparently intrinsic to human physiology to throw a ball and hit a ball, catch a ball, chase a grounder and miss the cutoff. In the mid-1800s teams represented cities and played one another. That was one new wrinkle, and after the Civil War there was another: professionals took over. One of them was a Philadelphia-born pitcher named Jim Devlin, who was born in obscurity in 1849 and died in oblivion in 1883. In between, he was a man of his century.

Devlin's education had been rudimentary. He was unsophisticated but well-liked, as he established a solid reputation as a pitcher. His trademark was the toothpick wagging around in his mouth while he played. Hired by the Louisville Grays, Devlin pitched 685 innings in his first full season, with an earned run average of 1.50. A pitcher with a pale version of those stats today is considered a beast and will receive at least $12 million per year. The word in that assessment that would have made Devlin jealous is not "million," however. It is "receive." In 1876 he was promised a fantastic amount of money, $2,000 a year. Except that the Louisville team abruptly stopped paying its players midway through the season. Devlin tried to switch to St. Louis, but thanks to rules instituted by the brand-new National League, he was bound to Louisville.

The world is not an excuse. However, the one in which Devlin arose to play ball was rife with cheats. The Brooklyn *Eagle* sports page welcomed the start of the 1877 season by reporting that every team in the fledgling National League was tainted with crooked players, with only one exception. The paper didn't blame the cheating players so much as the managers who hired them, time and again. "A man who will consent to sell a game lacks the honesty to keep faith with anyone," advised the paper. It concluded that the Boston team was the only one without any cheaters; a tribute to Boston coming from a Brooklyn paper was bound to be true. Games throughout the league were typically routs and because teams were so often mismatched, the most popular form of betting on baseball sidestepped the final score altogether.

Perhaps it is analogous to mention that whenever I have a particularly bad day at golf, the kind of afternoon when I shoot a neat 67—per hole—I start a separate score when I (finally) reach the green. If I hole out in two, by God, it's still a sport and a fine accomplishment. In one and my heart sings. In any case, I write the number of putts above all the many, many, many other numerals on my scorecard, giving new hope to a bad outing. In a similar way, baseball bettors in the 1870s separated out the competitive part of the game by focusing on one question: will the dominating team tally more runs in *any* two innings combined than the weaker one scores in the whole game? If the powerful Bumblebees—no matter their total score—boasted two innings that totaled five, while the wimpy Wasps had a final score of four, then bettors who put money on the

Bumblebees to "win in two innings" were jubilant. It could happen, however, that the Bumblebees won 9–3, doing so by scoring one run in each inning; then people betting on them to "win in two innings" would lose their bet: the combination of their best two innings was 2 and the Wasps made 3 altogether. Sometimes the bet was written for one inning or three innings, but usually it was two.

Should you ever find yourself in New York City in 1876, you will now know how to place a bet on baseball.

In the summer of 1876, a Brooklyn bookie by the name of Fred Seibert tried to enlist Jim Devlin in throwing a game or two. Seibert and his partner, a man named McCloud, conducted their business by placing ads in various columns of the New York *Herald*'s classified ads, listing the Manhattan street corner where they could be found that day, along with the games on which they'd be taking bets. Both changed by the day: the street corners, as well as the games. In order to increase profits, Seibert also made use of the telegraph lines, having instructed cheating ballplayers to send messages telling him when they planned to throw a game. For secrecy, the men were to use his list of "cipher words" for the opposing teams. For example, a player would send a wire to Seibert reading, "Buy Bertram to win in 3 innings" or "Buy Darling to win in 2 innings."

That unbreakable code, in which no living being could possibly discern a reference to baseball, indicates the level of the gambling operations that were undermining a magnificent sport. (For the record, "Bertram" meant Cincinnati; "Darling" was Louisville.) Another indication of the dubious elements aligned against honest baseball was the fact that Seibert's place of business on any given day was a crack in the sidewalk somewhere in lower Manhattan. And yet, after every thrown game, Seibert and McCloud did faithfully send the cheating players involved $100 or $200 in hard cash and on that, their business was thriving.

Devlin flatly rejected Seibert's 1876 overture to cheat with the Grays. The next year, though, on a road trip to New York City, he was introduced to McCloud by the newsstand operator at the hotel in which he was staying: no doubt a red-letter day for the newsseller. In Devlin's recollection, the gambler "said that when I wanted to make a little money to let him know. Was to use the word 'sash' in telegraphing him." Meanwhile, one of Devlin's Louisville teammates, George Hall, was also wavering. Hall's playing had always been straight, a fact that was causing problems in his family.

"My brother-in-law," Hall related, "has often said, 'I was a fool for not making money [throwing games].' He has said this for several years." Finally, Hall capitulated. He and a teammate cooperated with the gamblers and then, on a road trip to Ohio, he asked Devlin about cheating. In no time, a telegram with the word "sash" was delivered to McCloud.

With that, the Grays lost to Cincinnati...and then Indianapolis. And so on in the summer of '77. In Devlin's defense, cheating on baseball teams wasn't well-coordinated. Others on the Grays were also known or suspected to be manipulating the games. Then again, there was the opposing team and whatever its players were doing for T. E. Johnson, Kelly & Bliss, or whichever bookies *they* secretly worked for. The wonder is that anyone knew for sure which way to run on the bases. Whoever made it happen, however, the vaunted Grays blew an enormous lead in the standings and lost the pennant. An investigation followed.

None of that presented a new chapter in the short history of professional baseball. Players cheated, owners investigated, and, as the Brooklyn *Eagle* said, players "who have been dismissed from outside clubs for crooked play" joined the next team down the road. Following the usual script, Devlin humbly confessed, leaving out few if any details. Other suspected Grays did the same. Devlin then awaited his fate, anticipating that he'd be sacked from the Grays and go on to St. Louis, his heart's desire. He had reason for optimism when the matter was ultimately handed over to his good friend William Hulbert, the new president of the two-year-old National League. A bearish Chicagoan with a thriving brokerage, Hulbert, quite significantly, hadn't been involved in baseball before buying into the White Stockings as a civic gesture. To him, the Louisville scandal had absolutely nothing to do with friendship. On the contrary, it presented an opportunity "to strike an effective blow." With great fanfare, Hulbert expelled Devlin and the others—not just from the Grays, but from every team in the League and not just for the season, but forever.

That was it. Forever.

The others complained, but soon eased past baseball into regular jobs. As to Hall, it's fairly certain he never again sat next to his brother-in-law at Thanksgiving. Devlin, however, was affected more deeply. For two years, a man with subpar attainments in almost every field had been called the best of the best for something. It barely matters what it was, because as of December 15, 1877, it was gone. Though released from the narrow world of baseball into the wider world, Devlin responded as though he couldn't move: a fox in a trap, kicking out and writhing without ceasing, even though the only one he was hurting was himself. He tried to express the circumstances of his cheating and the ways that he was different, but when he did, he was using the language of all that he had known before. Baseball wasn't going to speak that language anymore. He swore that when he promised never to cheat again, he was telling the *absolute* truth. When it comes to cheating, though, truth isn't absolute—a fact that William Hulbert, for one, chose not to ignore.

Devlin wrote tortured letters to Hulbert for the rest of his life; every day, according to some reports. Often, he wrote to others, too, including Boston's manager, Harry Wright, asking for work of any kind, including on the groundskeeping crew—anything to be back in baseball:

> If you Can do me this favor By letting me take Care of the ground or anything of that Kind I Beg of you to do it and god will reward you if I Dont or let me Know if you have any Ide of how I Coed get Back I am Dumb Harry I don't Know how to go about it …

Albert Spalding, later known for his sporting goods company, started as a ballplayer and happened to be in Hulbert's outer office sometime after the scandal:

The outer door opened and a sorry-looking specimen entered. It was midwinter and very cold,
but the poor fellow had no overcoat. His dust-
covered garments were threadbare and seedy. His
shoes were worn through with much tramping,
while the red flesh showing in places indicated
that if stockings were present they afforded not
much protection...The visitor passed me without a glance in my direction. His eyes were
fixed upon the occupant of the farther room.
He walked straight to the chair where Mr. Hulbert sat, and, dropping to his knees at the big
man's feet, lifted his eyes in prayerful entreaty,
while his frame shook with the emotion so long
restrained...The man was Devlin, one of the
Louisville players. The situation, as he kneeled
there in abject humiliation, was beyond the
realm of pathos. It was a scene of heartrending
tragedy. Devlin was in tears, Hulbert was in tears,
and if the mists of a tearful sympathy filled my
eyes I have no excuse.

Hulbert pulled a fifty-dollar bill from his pocket,
gave it to Devlin, and with an eye grown steely sent him
away with the assurance that he could never and would
never be forgiven for having "sold a game." Devlin returned home to Philadelphia, where he kept on writing
letters to Hulbert. Living at poverty's very end, Devlin
died at thirty-three. Spalding was correct, the whole affair, all the way along, was a tableau of heartrending
tragedy; the only question was which kind.

In an aggravating movie called *Waterloo Bridge*, based

on a play by the otherwise respected Robert E. Sherwood, a virginal ballerina becomes engaged to a rich army officer and is thereupon thrown out of the ballet corps for thinking even for one *half* of one second about something other than ballet. Soon thereafter, when she is informed that the army officer has been killed in action, she has no livelihood. And so she becomes a prostitute. Of course! A streetwalker. She couldn't possibly just apply at Woolworth's.

One might think that, rather than shrivel up in abject poverty, Devlin also could have applied at Woolworth's. Or any other place that offered an honest wage. The fact that he fell so far so fast, however, was as useful for baseball executives as *Waterloo Bridge* was for ballet masters. Devlin's story was often told during the first twenty-five years of the National League. He provided the dividing line and if he didn't exactly die for the sins of baseball cheaters before and since, he certainly served as a vivid warning.

Devlin's case continues to present its mixture of triumph and regret. Because the rules, or their enforcement, changed under his feet, one is tempted to feel sorry for the poor guy. He was a martyr, but one of convenience, not conscience. Devlin was trapped by events rather than conviction. On that point, his fate was epic as his spirit toppled into dust. Devlin might have deserved pity, from history if not Hulbert—except that he threw League games. Some baseball cheaters at the time diddled exhibition games (of which there were many, in order to fill in a season), but never a League game. Moreover, Devlin could have confined himself to "win in two innings" types of tampering. He didn't have to throw everything: innings, games, League games, the pennant.

In the present day, Devlin is rarely remembered in baseball, but across the arc of cheating history, he lives on as the symbol of every honest effort to give a reset to the world (or any slice of it). He didn't get a second chance when he was caught because of the prevailing opinion that a cheater is stamped for life, unable to resist the temptation to betray again. Since the dawn of man, only two routes have been available to those wishing to start the world over as a haven free from cheating. The first is to get rid of the cheater. That was Hulbert's verdict for Devlin. The second route is to rehabilitate the cheater and offer another chance, if not three or four.

Elimination of the cheater is a controversial move. It seems drastic. And it is drastic. Losing hope on a person always is. The second option, that of redemption, is also hotly debated, because it requires placing faith in a cheater. That can be drastic, too—but not for the cheater. In practical terms, it will spread the fault the next time he or she slips up to anyone who extended that extra chance. Alternatively, it holds out the pride of munificence for those granting another chance. In a recent Super Bowl, the Most Valuable Player award (which has always seemed an oxymoron in any team sport, but that is beside the point), the MVP was a veteran player who had been suspended at the beginning of the season for blatant cheating in the use of a performance-enhancing drug (PED). His "comeback" was regarded as a feel-good story, publicized far and wide. William Hulbert, from a stance that held grown-ups accountable for their actions, would have been less forgiving. Acutely aware of the competitive nature of sports—not in winning games, but a place on a professional team—I might question how good the feeling is for the players who didn't make that or other teams, because they never took PEDs. Therein lies the second aspect of the redemption route, which is no less drastic for its being as quiet as the non-cheating would-be player who is sitting in his backyard while the Super Bowl is blaring on everybody else's TV.

The debate of rejection versus redemption, as a means of putting an end to a cheater's activities, was reflected in a survey of newspaper readers in Southern California. It showed that 56 percent held that a spouse who commits adultery should not be taken back after being caught, while 44 percent thought the spouse should "be given a second chance." The survey conveys a profound truth. Perhaps you noticed it: the two sides add up to 100 percent. Not one respondent checked "Don't know," "Not sure," "n.a.," "What's 'adultery'?" "What's 'second'?" "What's 'be'?" or even choice #8: "The adulterer should be taken back and branded with a big 'A,' not on the lapel, thank you, Mr. Hawthorne, but on the forehead, where it won't be mistaken for Anne Klein or Armani, especially after the blood dries and it scabs over and then becomes a shiny scar."

In truth, the survey on adulterers may be the first in the history of polling to add up to 100 percent. That total reveals that the single topic upon which every American has a distinct opinion is: Take the dirtball back or not? It isn't one of those nuanced questions, such as "Who was the first president of the United

States?" In recent surveys, that one has elicited between 12 and 75 percent "Don't know" replies.* Adultery, conversely, doesn't draw "Don't know" replies. It's demonstrably a topic to which people have given due consideration. While some may value the gifts of George Washington to the nation, everyone knows whether a spouse should slam the door on a cheater.

A woman in Missouri years ago spent her adult life around men who worked for the railroad or rode it regularly. Mrs. "Missouri," as she called herself, started her overview by describing a very typical type of wife, one who spent afternoons fooling around with a "sweetie" until the "husband's train whistles for the crossing." That left time for her to get dressed and slip back home "so hubby won't get suspicious."

A train whistle is never going to sound the same way again, of course. In fact, a train will never look the same. Only to the callow and the innocent could one appear to be a land-based locomotion vehicle. To women of the world, especially ones relegated to a small railroad town, they are devices for efficiently removing husbands. And they're equipped with city-wide alert systems to sound in advance of the husbands' return. A lot of brilliant engineering went into that invention in Scotland, England, and America. And according to Mrs. M., it worked.

The railroad was a different type of modern convenience for husbands, according to Mrs. M.: just the thing for collecting ladies of potential carnal interest, lining

* Rest easy: The 75 percent were high school students in a state where the boys' football teams have exceptionally lavish stadiums.

them up in seats, and separating them from the bounds of community. "There is a man with six babies [at home]," she wrote, "who goes down on the train each morning. He parades up and down 'looking them over' and then always tries to sit down by the one who looks the easiest.

"He has done so much chasing," Mrs. M. continued philosophically, "his face has lost all expression, a perfect blank. The same as his head." Like an oft-quoted character in a play at the time, she trusted "no man till I've seen him with a lily on his chest." To stop cheating spouses, Mrs. M. was the one who came up with the idea on page 167 of branding their foreheads—I cannot take credit for that innovation. (Though the show-offy reference to *The Scarlet Letter* and the oh-so-shocking use of the word "scab" were mine and mine alone.)

In defense of errant husbands, studies have shown that they are more likely than wives to break off an ongoing affair once caught. A University of Connecticut analysis based on anonymous records from over a hundred marriage counselors concluded that "wives are three times as likely as their husbands to continue." Notably, that refers to cheating in a single, specific relationship. Studies are uniformly pessimistic on the prospect of anything stopping spouses who compulsively parade "up and down 'looking them over.'"

Samantha Deming, a respected family counselor in Santa Clarita, California, created a test that seeks to predict in a general way whether a spouse caught cheating is likely to stop or continue. Her list reveals the factors involved in a complex process that determines whether a person *can* stop and then whether he or she *will* stop:

FIG. 11.1A—Test to Identify Chronic Cheaters and Whether a Spouse Who Has Strayed Will Do So Again

(Used by permission of Samantha Deming, M.A., Licensed Marriage and Family Therapist)

1. Was your spouse with someone else when you began your relationship with him/her?
2. Did you become involved before the other relationship ended?
3. Do you know about instances where your spouse cheated on another relationship?
4. Does your spouse tend to rationalize other "moral transgressions"?
5. Does your spouse believe that "What someone doesn't know won't hurt them"?
6. Is your spouse reluctant to give you information about where they will be, frequently?
7. Does your spouse blame you for the affair and not take personal responsibility?

As the first questions indicate, a marriage that begins in adultery has a fragile foundation for containing it. This was seen in the example in Chapter 5, in which a husband habitually looked to his present wife's best friend as a conquest and future wife. The next questions in Deming's test look for a sign that the person cares. Without that short but complicated word, the discussion of the future will have no leverage. The questions near the end of the list seek to identify the type of person who "compartmentalizes" life and feels that extramarital affairs are on the other side of a high wall from home and family. It's a wall, in most cases, that no one else can see. The last question, in particular, isolates the fourth type of chronic cheater, which is someone so manipulative that adultery is not merely an end, in and of itself, but a form of aggression.

FIG. 11.1B—Answer Key for Questions Above

Number of Questions to Which Betrayed Spouse Answered "Yes"	Probability of Future Affair by Errant Spouse (as assessed by experts)
2–3	It might be wise to look out for another possible affair.—*Deming*
4+	I would strongly consider your partner may have already established a pattern of cheating. A pattern is harder to change.—*Deming*
6	Which of you rides the train in Missouri every day?—*author*
7	Remember when your grandmother kept forgetting your name and called you *Mia Patetico Sciocco**? Your grandmother didn't forget your name.—*author*

* *Italian for grandmothers (of people bound to marry badly):*
Mia patetico sciocco—*"My pathetic sap"*

An Arkansas man who'd been married thirty years had his own opinion on the topic. "For a marriage to work," he explained, "you have to get beyond love as a feeling." He didn't have time to explain further, because he was about to be married, or remarried. He was heading to a stadium in Little Rock with his wife, to be wed along with thousands of other couples according to the tenets of "covenant marriage," which, he said, "can help you find that spiritual love."

The covenant marriage was initiated in 2005–2006 in Louisiana, Arkansas, and Arizona. The concept is that regular marriage isn't being taken very seriously, especially in the South, where divorce rates are typically twice those in other regions. Couples presenting themselves at a clerk's office are therefore given the choice of abiding by standard laws of marriage (and divorce) or stepping up to a stricter level. The covenant marriage requires counseling in advance of a wedding and/or potential divorce, and also specifies narrow grounds for divorce. Incompatibility isn't one of the grounds and neither is mental duress. Neither is overhearing your husband say that for a marriage to work, you have to get beyond love as a feeling. Adultery, however, is on the list, which was a significant concession for couples absolutely intent on adhering to their marriage vows. Unlike, for example, committing murder and getting the death penalty—which is another of the acceptable grounds for divorce—adultery is a choice that is inextricably linked to the marriage. One might respectfully argue that not even the framers of the covenant marriage, high-minded as they no doubt were, could figure out a way to induce, force, or coerce both members of a couple to keep their paws off other people. When adultery does occur in a covenant marriage, however, mandatory therapy injects the hope of ending the cheating for good, before a divorce is granted. The inclination of the covenant law, in other words, is redemption over rejection.

In the same vein, but with a more severe bearing, is the honor code used in many institutions, notably colleges and, most notably, military academies. It also spells out the consequences of cheating well in advance, but typically opts for rejection of the cheater, first-time or any time. The usual process is for the new arrival to read the honor code in the presence of some counselor or official, in order to ensure that every aspect is absorbed and understood. The code is then signed and dated.

The debate about whether a cheater can be stopped and how best to accomplish it was carried out poignantly among strangers in Florida, in response to the summary expulsion of a student who violated the University of Florida's honor code. At the time, the campus was roiled by concerns that academics at the proud institution were secondary to its athletic program. If that statement narrows the possible timeframe hardly at all, neither does the description of the newly elected captain of the football team, who, it was said, "has heard nothing of the over-emphasis of football at the Gainesville institution, knows nothing about it other than what he has read in the newspapers, and furthermore, is not contemplating any serious investigation of the matter. He's more interested in the Gators' outlook in next year's...conference football."

The football captain, Carlos Proctor, a star tackle from Tampa, was a legend even as a freshman for playing most of one hard-fought Gators game while blood blinded him in one eye. Proctor was voted captain of the team as a sophomore, an unusual honor. For a natural athlete who was fairly obsessed with football, the outlook for conference football was sublime. All that he had to do was finish the spring semester and then move on to beating the Bulldogs of the University of Georgia and other such autumn projects. Instead, at the end of March, he resigned from the university and went home. That month, Proctor had been caught cheating during a test for his political science course. Less than ten days later, his fellow students on the Honor Court tried his case. By the time they voted to expel him, he was already long gone. For him, the football season ended in March. The case was straightforward: an honor code had succeeded in removing a cheater. The same newspapers that printed his exploits on the gridiron carried the news of his expulsion. In Florida, it was front-page news.

Francis Bellamy, a Tampa resident, was incensed. "What, under Heaven, was the need of identifying him and ruining his business prospects in Tampa forever?...Most unhappily the yielding to the temptation of cheating in scholastic examinations is a very prevalent weakness, and has been ever since examinations began. While drastic penalties of expulsions have been given to the detected ones, they are no more guilty than great numbers of their fellow students. As a matter of fact, who hasn't at one time or another cheated at some examination?" Bellamy's overall rationale is a common one, with his argument that everyone—in whatever pursuit—cheats. The implication that follows is that no one person should be punished for what everyone does. (I have long wished that that attitude would prevail among police officers toward speeders.)

"He is old enough to know right from wrong, isn't he?" snapped another Tampa resident. "If considered 'unfortunate' and that he made a 'mistake' wouldn't he do it again because he got off light? Certainly." Her feelings about the potential for transforming a cheater were clear, if pessimistic: "A child can be taught before even going to school that cheating is a form of stealing. This done effectively, there would be fewer occupying the jails." According to her, Proctor's episode could not be isolated. If he cheated as a student, he would certainly do so as an adult, especially if he were not stopped cold.

Another woman, Janet Sellars, was outraged by that stand. Ominously, she started by insinuating that the previous letter writer couldn't possibly be a mother with children in school. If one is tempted to ask why not—and don't all parents teach their kids "even before going to school that cheating is a form of stealing"?—the answer is no. Many mothers and fathers sidestep that lesson, but very few have as supple a relationship with ethics as Mrs. Sellars. As a nurse, a teacher, and a mother, she agreed with Bellamy that nobody's perfect in regard to cheating. What is more, she claimed she had never seen a student who would not "cheat an examination when it became necessary to do so in order to make marks on their report cards they were not ashamed to show." As quickly as possible, we'll glance at the other possibility, in which the *cheated* report card is the one that makes a child ashamed. And now back to Mrs. Sellars: "I have seen," she wrote, "another type far worse than the cheater—the type who would cheat and then lie about it."

For those who grew up in a different type of household, one in which any kid who cheated would be instantly electrocuted by the look in their parents' eyes, Mrs. Sellars's contemplations on ethics are vexing. If little Bess received all Cs and Ds, but did so without any help, her mother regarded her as a stain on the family escutcheon. The embarrassment, the bitter regret. If she got all As, however, cheated first to last and said so, she was a paragon of virtue, with her photograph in the living room. But if she cheated and then lied about it, insisting that her stellar grades were honestly earned, her mother would shake her head and say that she just didn't understand right and wrong.

I can't follow it, either—except to say that Mrs. Sellars confirms one thing: There are people in the background in any picture of a cheater. And they may very well say that you, not the perpetrator, are the one who should be ashamed.

As to Carlos Proctor, he turned from college football directly to professional boxing, compiling a record of two wins by knockout and no losses. He quickly came to regard pro boxing as a festival of cheating. His last bout was stopped because his opponent was so obese and inept that they were both dragged out of the ring by the fans and then thrown out of the arena. Understandably disgusted, Proctor reverted to college sports, which he coached without particular distinction for about a dozen years. He was later named to the University of Florida's Athletic Hall of Fame. Proctor, whose life spanned across the twentieth century, was much more the modern man than Devlin. He was rejected but only temporarily. Moreover, he had from first to last fans on his side, who couldn't mention his name or tell his story without claiming that he—the one who cheated—got a raw deal. He was described by one admirer as "a pilgrim, kicked by fate off the summit of success."

The introduction of fate as an element in cheating is another means of alleviating blame on the cheater. But "fate" refers to the impact of unseen events. Cheating is invariably a matter of self-determination. Proctor was a charismatic fellow and he made up for his cheating as well as anyone could, throughout the rest of his life, but he acted of his own volition during the spring of his freshman year. Kind of nice or utterly destructive, cheaters have one thing in common: an abject distrust of fate. Even a fear of it.

CHAPTER 12

Section Two Conclusion

You. Who Cheat

Love means many things, most of which are well re-flected by music. Probably, the two entities emerged on the very same day, a long time ago: love and music. Adultery, on the other hand, was largely banished from music, especially popular music in America. Country music discovered that oversight in 1948, when a song called "One Has My Name" was a hit. With its lament reflected in the line "To one I am tied, to the other I am true," it quickly became a stan-dard in the genre. Having tripped onto the void for songs about affairs, country music rushed to fill it. One duo, the Kendalls, made a career writing sordid little ditties, such as the immortal "You'd Make an Angel Want to Cheat," along with "It Don't Feel Like Sinnin' to Me," "Teach Me to Cheat," "Pittsburgh Stealers," "Plain Old-Fashioned Cheatin'," and their signature song, "Heaven's Just a Sin Away."

Because cheatin' and sinnin' have been the bedrock

of country music for generations, listeners hear such songs all day, every day, on the radio, through streaming services or from their own collection. It has often been considered brainwashing. The program director of a country station in Miami admitted that when cheating songs topped the charts, which was often, "The station will get a lot of calls from women saying that the songs make their husbands think about cheating."

It would make most people think of writing a song about cheating. All it seems to require is four words or less, preferably cliché-ridden. "Pittsburgh Stealers." Honestly. I could think of a more hackneyed song title in five seconds, if that's what they want.

"Detroit Lyin's."

There. Four seconds.

The wives of Miami needn't have worried: People do not commit adultery because of cheating songs, at least not in droves, as though the thought of an affair would never have occurred to a philanderer without "Heaven's Just a Sin Away" drumming through his ears. If the collected works of the Kendalls apply to anything in their literal sense, it would not be love and marriage. In the heat of the moment, it would be basketball.

Looking at the strategy of the game, as played at the college level, a college head coach earns on average about $5 million per year for recruiting seventeen-year-old boys to transfer a playground game to a huge arena. The boys are strictly forbidden from earning anything, starting with the very first recruiting letter sent to them and ending with graduation or the NBA draft or a less ceremonious day when they drop out, no longer eligible, no longer needed. To reiterate, the coach desperately needs a handful of teenage boys to earn his millions of dollars. The school needs them to reap their tens of millions of dollars. And in a newer development, apparel and sneaker companies need the same handful of talented kids in order to gain their hundreds of millions of dollars. For a time, it seemed sleazy enough that contracts bound whole colleges to one sweatshirt maker or sneaker company, to the exclusion of all others. Then the manufacturers seeded the clouds, finding ways to steer promising high schoolers to the college teams wearing the right tags.

With money raining down, callous barracudas circle every callow, if tall, recruit, just as though their lives depended on him. The scenario that plays out daily across America is the stuff of glory, pathos, and Italian opera. Because the result is unsurprising, however, its sense of tragedy pulled down to the mundane, it is better suited to country music.

"TEACH ME TO CHEAT"

In the late 1970s, Reggie Carter was a high-scoring guard from New York City. He was pursued by schools in the Northeast, but the offer he accepted was from the one farthest away: the University of Hawaii. The difference was with the assistant who did the recruiting, a charismatic former college player in one of his first coaching posts. "I was recruited by Rick Pitino," Carter recalled, "and I figured he knew when he said everything was legit."

"HEAVEN'S JUST A SIN AWAY"

Because of the distance between New York City and Hawaii, Pitino arranged for airplane tickets for Carter. Schools were forbidden from underwriting travel by the National Collegiate Athletic Association, but Carter was supposed to earn the money for his fares with a summer job. When the job didn't quite materialize, the athletic department continued to provide transportation.

"IT DON'T FEEL LIKE SINNIN' TO ME"

On arriving for his freshman year in Hawaii, Carter couldn't obtain a room in a dorm, so he was encouraged to take an off-campus apartment. Because rents on the islands were high, he couldn't handle his living expenses on the amount allowed by the NCAA. He could afford either room or board, but not both. The coaching staff gave him money for the latter, an impulse of generosity or expedience that was forbidden according to the rules.

"PLAIN OLD-FASHIONED CHEATIN' "

Carter's apartment was not just off-campus, it was a long hike away. Encouraged by the coaches, the frosh player sold the pair of season tickets he'd been allotted and used the proceeds to buy a car. No one told him that was wrong or suggested he read the *NCAA Division*

I Manual, which specifically bans schools from providing cars and athletes from selling tickets.

"YOU'D MAKE AN ANGEL WANT TO CHEAT"

When the NCAA investigated the Hawaii basketball program in 1977, Reggie Carter was branded as a cheater and forced to leave school. "That was a year of my life," he said when he was back in New York City again. "When you're hit with something like this, it just depresses you. People remember the bad things and they won't let you forget. It slows you up, and you just can't shake it." The Hawaii head coach, who was later banned from the game for life, said of Carter, "He's suffered the most. I suppose we let him down in a way." Pitino said much the same thing, admitting that "before Reggie came to Hawaii, he was definitely not a cheater."

The happy ending of the story lies entirely with Carter. After a year of suspension, he found a haven at St. John's University in New York City, where he had a stellar career. He later played in the professional ranks with the Knicks. After that, he devoted his working life to teaching and administrative posts in public schools, including Mineola High School on Long Island. Carter died of a heart attack in 1999, but Mineola remembers "his character, his work ethic and what he stood for" every year with a scholarship, a memorial basketball game, and the Carter Awards for students exhibiting his qualities. People didn't "remember the bad things" at all.

Pitino went on to a storied career as a coach in college basketball, notably at the University of Kentucky. A later stint at the University of Louisville, however, ended in October of 2017 with his termination by the board of trustees. On his watch, players were given more than plane tickets: Prostitutes were made available, even on campus. The school was also charged with paying players. In addition, an apparel maker was accused of discussing a bribe with the father of a top recruit. As a result of the most egregious scandal in college basketball history, five years' worth of achievements by the team, including the national championship of 2013, were revoked. Pitino, who proclaimed his innocence in the charges, was permanently linked with cheating. And yet he was rumored two years later to be looking at a return to college coaching. One of the schools said to interest him most was St. John's University.

In a similar vein, the apparel maker charged in the Louisville maelstrom has continued to solidify its place in college basketball and in the lives of the players. The top recruit whose father discussed money with the company never played a day in college basketball, nor was he drafted by the NBA. His reputation in this country having been ruined, he signed with an Australian team.

In an article about Pitino for the *New York Times*, Victor Mather observed: "When success comes with scandal, people often pay more attention to the success." That is the fact of modern times, but not just in sports. Whether one is bitter about that fact or delighted with it depends on just two points. The first, of course, is whether one can see what has been lost. And next, how well can one keep from looking in that direction?

Cheating and a Society That Likes It

CHAPTER 13

Your America Today

Cheaters Always Win

When John Winthrop and his fellow Puritans neared the shores of the Massachusetts Bay Colony early in the summer of 1630, they were naturally excited to be starting anew. Winthrop, an intensely devout man, called the flock together to deliver a layman's sermon on that very topic: their new society. All were determined to create a better life for the community at large, to turn a fresh page on the old attitudes in England according to any design they chose. One might think that Winthrop's talk would be all about worship, God, and churchly matters. Puritans had that reputation. Those topics had been covered, though—almost incessantly since the group banded together. In any case, in terms of a plan for their colony, any announcement to the effect of "because we are God's best children, everything is going to be jake" hands off the responsibility. Winthrop had his faults, but he was no shirker. He looked down at the actual fresh page—the one on which he was going to write his sermon just as soon as he thought of it. Meanwhile, with each slap of water on the hull of the boat, an epoch was waiting.

Winthrop was specifically concerned with the divide between the rich and the poor, "as in all times some must be," he observed. He was deeply afraid that in the rare chance called America, the two groups would accomplish little except to cheat one another. It wasn't exactly an original thought; Winthrop sprang from England, the nation that coined the very word.

The legal term was "escheat," which was based on the Latin, *excadere*, meaning "to fall away." The English crown used the word to describe its right to absorb any property that was not properly probated, or transferred to legal heirs. If a commoner died with a farm and no heirs, the "escheater," being the representative of the royal family, would come around and the farm would "fall away" to the king or the queen. If a commoner had both a farm and rightful heirs, but died without a sturdy will, the same would happen. The escheaters gained their reputation, though (and the populace dropped the "es-" in the word), when someone had a farm, heirs, *and* a sturdy will—and the property went to the crown anyway. The royal family would often then hand it over to some local rich person who had been useful in politics or war. The English people were too spirited to accept such treatment for very long, making their history rife with conflict and scenery irresistible to video game designers.

Winthrop was determined to leave England's torn scenery behind. His primary hope was that if emigrants could start fresh, once and for all, then the many means of cheating as a form of power would be unknown to their new society. "What rule must we observe?" he asked rhetorically in his sermon. "The same as before, but with more enlargement towards others and lesse respect towards ourselves and our owne right." He laid out the "covenant" as he called it, asserting that if the Puritans were good to one another, then the civilization to come would be—in his most famous phrase—"as a citty upon a hill," admired and emulated by others.

Winthrop's group of Puritans have often been described as having sailed to America to find religious freedom, but as they prepared to disembark from the boat, Winthrop was even more nervous about matters of—as it were—the other six days in the week. He was obviously not only tired of all the old rules, but also the myriad ways his former countrymen had devised for breaking them in order to get ahead. In a typical sentiment from the sermon, he proposed that "sensibleness and sympathy of each other's conditions will necessarily infuse into each parte a native desire and endeavour, to strengthen, defend, preserve and comfort the other." The colony, in other words, was founded on freedom, all right: freedom from chiseling.

"The common corruptions of this evill world," as John Winthrop expressed it.

Winthrop had taken his best shot at an exercise that went back a long, long way: convincing a community to start fresh. On any excuse to pivot, leaders of a certain sort have implored people to stop treating one another shabbily, including in large measure the everyday betrayal: cheating. Through preceding centuries, some prophets proffered threats of heavenly retaliation, some pointed to role models (such as saints), some relied on xenocentricity ("those people over there cheat; we don't"), and so on through every opportunity to start fresh and live *with more enlargement toward others*. The most common impetus of all is geographical. A subset of people move to their own spot, their own new world. The Puritans did just that.

As Winthrop sat on the boat, looking at the blank piece of paper that awaited his plan for an incorruptible society, he was the picture of all others who have tried to imagine, at long last, an effective answer to the oldest of questions: What can you do with people? How can they be scared, bribed, beaten, or inspired into being fair and square? Every means of coaxing has been tried with only wavering success, in terms of permanent reengineering.

In Winthrop's case, the exhortation for compassion among the newly arrived Puritans did lead to an atmosphere of decency, at least for a few years. After that, the "sensibleness and sympathy of each other's conditions" faded. The relapse to a more recognizable, more cheating society didn't result from any dramatic trend. It came when the spirit of passion for the newly created society was eroded by more immediate, individual concerns.

To continue this monograph on "Fresh Pages in Our Nation's History," the next attempt to inveigle Americans to straighten up came with the founders. After they wrestled the (loosely) united (bunch of) states into a country, it became clear to them that they had unleashed a wild force of nature—a mob of humans—with no countervailing queen, khan, koenig, empress, or shah. Turning a nation over to "the people" had been catchy as a rallying cry. Once it actually happened, the leaders of the Revolution were acutely aware of who was likely to ruin the whole thing: the people. The abiding message from them was that a democratic republic depended on the people adopting a new national character. There would be no other whip hand. A consensus of honest behavior on the part of every citizen was the only support beneath a democracy. Benjamin Franklin's *Autobiography*, published posthumously and reaching American readers in 1793, included an account of his youthful effort to arrive at "moral perfection." The section was soon lifted out of the rest of the book and widely published first in periodicals and then separately as Franklin's *Art of Virtue*. The list included #7, Sincerity: "Use no harmful deceit..." Franklin, like any master analyst of human ethic, also employed charts.

"Public virtue" was the term George Washington often used. The year he was inaugurated president, he wrote of the "felicity" that he hoped would be permanent in the new country. "I think I see a *path*," he wrote, "as clear and direct as a ray of light, which leads to the attainment of that object. Nothing but harmony, honesty, industry and frugality are necessary to make us a great and happy people. Happily the present posture of affairs and the prevailing disposition of my countrymen promise to co-operate in establishing those four great and essential pillars of public felicity." Eight years later, on leaving office, Washington reiterated the interrelationship of good government and honest citizenship, declaring in his Farewell Address that "the foundations of our national policy will be laid in the pure and immutable principles of private morality."

Public virtue and good citizenship were common references in the Young America era. The tale of Washington and the cherry tree (in which he admitted to his angry father that he had chopped down a valuable tree) may have been apocryphal, invented whole cloth by a later biographer, but Washington would have appreciated the theme nonetheless. American liberty required honesty. However, as the country became increasingly money-mad in the early 1800s, pettiness, mendacity, get-rich-quick schemes, and greed in general corroded the four pillars of Public Virtue. Yet another fresh start was required.

One was at hand, as Americans in the 1830s and 1840s made a veritable fad of the latest way to turn the page. Starting a religion.

Anyone could start a religion and many did, sometimes attributing their ideas to divine inspiration and sometimes proudly taking full credit for themselves. For a reason that is hard to pinpoint, much of the yearning for a clean sweep in the nation's morality arose in central and western New York State. Spiritualism, Mormonism, and Adventism originated there, along with dozens, if not hundreds, of religions less well known today, including, for example, Millerism, which promised that the Second Coming of Christ would occur in 1843. After a hurried recalculation later that year, the date was set for 1844. In 1845, everybody quit Millerism. The religion market—if it can be called that, with due respect—was constantly churning, new entries cropping up or folding all over the region. Because it was easy to leave one religion and switch to another, start-ups were typically welcomed by adherents in the mood for something new.

The commitment was much higher for a related way to turn a new page: Association. It was an influential concept, which was also based largely in upstate New York. A landed gentleman from Batavia, New York, Albert Brisbane, was one of those who popularized it. He was disgusted in particular by the effect of business fraud:

> Although its universal practice has in a measure legalized it, still it cannot be considered in any other light than a rude and selfish impulse of the individual to cheat and defraud for the purpose of personal gain. It is one of the most glaring examples of the universal conflict of interests, which at present exists, and which will one day cease fully in Association.

"Association" referred to a commune, a self-contained settlement based on a utopian vision. Associations set up rules of their own, sometimes in the name of religion and sometimes in loathing rejection of it, but all in the optimism that people wouldn't break rules that offered them a better society. Two in particular promised an immediate end to adultery. For the Shakers, the answer was celibacy. For the Oneida

Community, it was free love with lots of babies. It's easy to guess which one lasted longer.

The Shakers. By design, they continually recruited new adherents, who thought that life in a Shaker community was intriguing. Shakerism has lasted over two hundred years, explained by its favorite hymn, "Tis a Gift to Be Simple." The Oneida Community, on the other hand, only lasted about thirty years, until 1880. By then, the younger generation in the Community thought that the free love of their parents' generation was all right for old people, but it was dullsville for youngbloods. They wanted to do their own thing, which was to get married and settle down.

Most of the other utopian communes of the 1840s were focused less on relationships and more on economic factors. And they did a cynic proud. Within a year or two, someone was heard to bellow, "Get your stinking hands off my communal property!" Or something to that effect. As soon as the dust settled, everyone would take something they'd always wanted and leave for home. Paradoxically, the communes of the 1840s likewise warmed the hearts of idealists. They could see within them that a strong appetite existed for a peaceable kingdom of humans, one that erased those lines of selfishness that lead to everyday betrayal. Communes as a solution to that problem faded, though, after the original hope for them died out. Even with the best of intentions, they rarely worked, except as experiments in instant improvement. Their only resurgence came within the counterculture movement of the late 1960s and early 1970s. That era seemed intent on throwing out the old and turning a fresh page, led by "a whole generation with a new explanation," according to John Phillips's song "San Francisco." Propelled and yet distracted by opposition to the Vietnam War, though, the movement dissipated when the last American troops finally came home.

During the first years of the Internet in the 1990s, it was touted as a place apart: a new kind of utopia. "When it was small enough not to have been noticed by criminals, it was a wonderful time," recalled Sir Tim Berners-Lee, who is credited as being the inventor of the Internet. He thought it would be a dramatically improved version of the real world. "Peer-to-peer" was predicted to be the basis of its power. Even as it became commercialized, much to Berners-Lee's dismay, fans predicted that the Internet would still "harmonize humanity," while downsizing, if not eradicating, monstrous corporations and sleazy businesses. In those early, egalitarian days, fuddy-duddies wondered how companies could possibly afford to create so much content for their websites, free for the surfing. They soon found out. Once the Internet became entrenched, it didn't look like a place apart, but a magnifying mirror of the real world. Fuddy-duddies and fans alike learned that no one loved that place apart more than corporations and businesses that were far more monstrous and even more sleazy than before.

The current century hasn't witnessed any notable inclination to raise the ethical standard of Americans. It has, however, offered sober warnings to anyone who presumes to so much as broach the topic. It is a dangerous undertaking.

FIG. 13.1—Free Association Transcript

In which a jaded modern American says the first thing that comes to mind when Person A endeavors to lead the nation to turn a fresh page:

	Moderator: I'd like to introduce Person A, who will discuss improving American ethics and tell us all why we shouldn't cheat anymore. Please say the first thing that comes into your head.
Person A:	**Modern American:**
It all comes down to this: "Do unto others as you would have them do unto you."	Plagiarizer.
Be *better* than you think you are.	Identity thief.
Dig down deep!	Televangelist.
Read Aristotle. Read Plutarch and Plato. Read Socrates.	Whatever the ancient Greek word for "flimflammer" is.
Even a little improvement to each day's activities adds up.	Bill padder.
So there you have it: all the rules you need to induce America to stop cheating.	Short shipper.

	Moderator: I'd like to introduce Person A, who will discuss improving American ethics and tell us all why we shouldn't cheat anymore. Please say the first thing that comes into your head.
Because the more often you can be that better person, the more you can say, "Yes. Yes, that *was* big of me."	Big o' me. Bingo.
Thank you.	Last-word freak.

In 1993, a volume called *The Book of Virtues* was published. The title had a certain Old Testament ring to it, which moved the eyes of skeptics immediately to the byline. Was it Solomon? Ezra? Nehemiah? It was William Bennett, a fixture in Washington political circles. The content of the book was a collection of previously published stories and folktales about people behaving admirably. After an astonishing eighty-eight weeks on the *New York Times* adult bestseller list, it went on to tally more than 2.2 million sales in its first four years. On the subject of responsibility, for example, all four stanzas of this 1833 poem were featured prominently in *The Book of Virtues*:

Three little kittens lost their mittens;
And they began to cry,

"Oh, mother, dear,
We very much fear
That we have lost our mittens."
"Lost Your Mittens!
You Naughty Kittens!
Then you shall have no pie!"
"Mee-ow, mee-ow, mee-ow"
"No, you shall have no pie."
"Mee-ow, mee-ow, mee-ow"

The three little kittens found their mittens;
And they began to cry,
"Oh, mother dear,
See here, see here!
See, we have found our mittens!"
"Put on your mittens,
You silly kittens,
And you may have some pie."
"Purr-r, purr-r, purr-r
Oh, let us have the pie!
Purr-r, purr-r, purr-r." [etcetera]

For eighty-eight weeks, authors throughout America existed in a state of numbed bewilderment.

The Book of Virtues formed the basis of a cascade of other books and products, with Bennett being called "a cottage industry of character education." He lectured widely on the topic of virtue and his name became something of a byword for either a sincere moralist or a holier-than-thou blowhard. Then, in 2003, the other shoe dropped, as it always does for moralists in our America. Shocking headlines appeared.

Investigative journalism revealed that Bennett was a high-stakes gambler, dropping hundreds of thousands of dollars at a sitting. *Washington Monthly* magazine called him the "Bookie of Virtues," though his activities were legal and had nothing to do with bookmaking. He played slot machines and video poker in parlors reserved at major casinos for high rollers seeking a measure of privacy.

"By furtively indulging in a costly vice that destroys millions of lives and families across the nation," wrote Joshua Green in *Washington Monthly*, "Bennett has profoundly undermined the credibility of his word on this moral issue." That socked it right to Bennett, as Green seized the moral high ground. How indeed could Bennett presume to censure three little kittens when he himself had lost his mittens. Along with his shirt. In the aftermath, he tacitly admitted to some shame by promising in public never to gamble again. The toppling of Bennett was soul-satisfying, both to those to whom he was a moralist and to those who thought him a foghorn.

That left Green. Felling Bennett set him up as the new face of righteousness. No doubt a fine man of unimpeachable character.

But did someone say something about vice undermining credibility on a moral issue? Wasn't it Green who said that? It made our ears prick up.

Did this Mr. Green never play Michigan rummy for real pennies? Did he never buy a raffle ticket at the Polish Home—or play New Penny Falls at an arcade in England? Did he never look under a box top to see if he won some kind of a dinosaur? Could any hominid possibly have lived hereabouts without indulging in a vice that destroys millions of lives? Did the man never watch TV?

How about beer? Yes, what about beer? Even one sip would profoundly undermine Green's credibility on moral issues. So says this gin drinker. The *Las Vegas Business Press* also grew suspicious, looking into the moral turpitude of the man who would topple the nation's previous authority on virtue. In an interview, Green admitted to a reporter at the *Business Press* that he thought Bennett had become a "national scold." That reporter investigated and found that Green had been given information on a whole range of celebrated plungers at the casinos, but that the only one he had dragged out into the glare of the desert sun was Bennett. Green quickly tried to explain the selective nature of his wrath, specifying that the *Virtues* author was the only one who "threw stones while living in a glass house." Poor Green. He didn't realize that he'd wandered into a neighborhood where they were all glass houses. Even his. The Las Vegas reporter was thus left alone on the field: standing in judgment of Green who stood in judgment of Bennett who stood in judgment of kittens.

If you now expect a complete rundown on that reporter, then I have made my point. And if that never occurred to you, then we are going to move on anyway, having covered the point to the satisfaction of everyone else that only a total dunderhead would tell Americans to turn a fresh page and stop cheating.

And yet.

If ever a country needed a fresh page, it is this

one now. America has always been witness to shabby ethics in some form, but never has cheating been so blithely accepted by the non-cheater and never has it been granted as a privilege of leadership, as it is today. On seeing the nation slipping down this steep precipice, the complete dunderhead, as we have seen, would say in response, "So therefore, don't cheat, anymore," and would instantly be bowled over by the chorus that is always at the ready: "But *you* cheat, *you* cheat, *you* cheat."

The three little kittens always repeated their raw emotion three times.*

A twenty-first-century observer might analyze the state of American ethics even more carefully, though, and sidestep the temptation to tell cheaters anything. In the first place, if George Washington couldn't get the message through to them, then nobody could. In the second place, even the greatest of leaders can only change about 75 percent of the people by about 12 percent. An individual, conversely, can change about twelve people by 75 percent. The key is to remind individuals of that power, while wondering how they could have forgotten it during the course of such a short time.

The better message for the era at hand is directed at non-cheaters: "Stop letting the cheaters get away with it." What counter-accusation can undercut that? It is a line of reasoning that keeps all concerned on

---

* You may have just noticed that this book has referred an inordinate number of times to the three little kittens who lost their mittens. I'm trying to get it to be a bestseller.

topic, impervious as it is to the charge of hypocrisy, that strong-arm of the status quo.

On topic, then, the national character currently at large is unique across the span of American history. It contends that there is something more important than integrity. That word marks a line, on the other side of which is cheating. The examples in this book and possibly those in your memory recall that getting caught on the wrong side of that line was until fairly recently a life-changing event. The people associated in some way with the cheater cared enough to make his or her life a gruesome misery. Not to wax nostalgic, but getting caught cheating meant getting in serious trouble; by definition that meant that society, in its flesh and blood form, would react; people beyond those who had been directly cheated took offense. Up until the last decade, society, whether in that smaller sense or on the largest scale, could be counted on, at least outwardly, to leave the impression that nothing was more important than integrity. That slipped when something became more important.

If that *something* that is more important were the same for everybody, then one could simply rail against it and declare victory. The sporting fact, though, is that the blank is filled in individually, reflecting a variety of perceived imperatives. As a result, honesty is relegated to a wide and growing place as a second priority in the American national character. The sense is not that it's been abandoned altogether, but that it can wait. Because first...the right team has to win, the most advantageous judges have to be appointed, the right company has to show a profit, the town has to be impressed with the right family. When the urgent matter at hand has been settled, then, according to the new mind-set, integrity will still be there, just as always. This theory has been tested myriad times in international history. It has appeared so often that a template to nurture it along has developed in every pursuit, from world domination on down. According to the template, it is well to provide an urgent priority if one doesn't occur naturally. However it happens, once people stop worrying about cheaters, one will invariably ascend. Did you ever wonder where—in the middle of a cold winter—a fruit fly could be lurking in your kitchen, biding his time, catching up on his reading, until the moment you let an apple on the counter get soft and then there he is, having a fruit fly party with all his friends? It's not the fruit fly's fault.

In this case, though, the fruit fly didn't cajole you into buying too many apples and then forgetting to eat them. He just sits there and...I don't know what he does. Returning quickly from entomology, the fact worth noting is that given a ripe environment, a cheater will likewise come from nowhere to take advantage. If not one cheater, then another.

The non-cheating population is of more interest, specifically those who overlook cheating. As a break with previous Americans, their advent is almost epidemic in its suddenness, its contagiousness, and its stealth. Factors that caught up to that population during our time, however, were a long time in the making.

When our society replaced an abiding respect for elders with a fascination for youth culture, a constant strain of guilt, shame, and self-hatred lifted. But at what cost?

The disapproving voice of a great-great-grandfather, even one whom you never met, was not only a guiding presence on wrong and right—and wrong again—but it was also an empowering force. Even in absentia, he could play the bad cop, as in, "Geez, Bucky, I really wouldn't care if you had a second family in Estonia— and a third in Taiwan—but Gramps Jervis would *tan my hide* if he knew I was friends with you. He brooked no tomcatting for married men, I tell you! Also, you're off the paintball team." The inclination to be cool with any interesting young person rather than Gramps Jervis has liberated the present wave of adults in America, but it has also removed a useful arrow from the quiver. America should have thought of that when it traded in ancestor worship for descendant worship.

A second factor reflects the way that noncheaters today were meticulously trained to allow cheating by others. It is contained in a single little phrase that represented a veritable mother lode for cheaters, present and future. The phrase was "Gets along well with others," and it was included on report cards.

> "What on earth business is it of the school's whether a kid gets along with others?"
>
> —Gramps Jervis

Without diverting to a monograph on the history of report cards in America, the present study will elucidate the general fact that before World War II, students were graded on all of the usual subjects, along with a line or two for the evaluation of characteristics such as "Is Polite" or "Exhibits Good Manners" and "Controls Temper." No one wants a hellion in class or in society as a whole, of course. After the war, a growing section of report cards included personality traits that went beyond etiquette, however, crossing a chasm to relationship. This was an insidious advance. Importantly, it negated the little person's right to form judgments. The line should read "Gets along well with others *who are not creeptown cheaters or rip-off whackos*." Just what would be wrong with a student who was unstintingly polite but didn't suffer schemers gladly? The discouragement of such discretion regarding people decreases inner toughness.

Today's adults are hobbled by a related reason to abstain from denouncing a cheater, especially one in the public sphere: The twenty-first century's adults have been stretched to the very limit on the subject of "cool." Marketing wizards raised them from the crib to be nothing less. The belief that you are what you buy is probably the reason that so few bother with developing a "philosophy of life."† They don't have to develop one when they can pick one up at the store.

---

† See chapter 9

FIG. 13.2—An Open Letter to the Postmaster General
of the United States:

Sir:

How are you? I am fine.

In the past, the country's first-class stamps have commemorated subjects not quite worthy of a museum on the Mall, yet diverting nonetheless: some overlooked doctor who cured every known disease, or a battle that accomplished absolutely nothing, but for which you had good art. Of late, however, I note that you have moved in a different direction, issuing stamps for relics plucked from utter American obscurity—such as Hot Wheels. *Star Trek. Sesame Street.* Disney cartoons and Wonder Woman. Scooby-Doo.

Please don't think I don't appreciate the good you are doing. These are playthings created by tiny companies that never quite achieved the success that was their due. Kudos to the U.S. government for helping them out.

Such stamps undeniably have an appeal for today's stamp-buying adults. Seeing them on an envelope evokes memories of all the crap spread out on the floor in their bedrooms when they were growing up. I am perfectly aware, as you obviously are, that there is something rather infantile about today's adults. The president of Facebook dresses as though Mrs. Cleaver bought his clothes. Hamburgers and French fries are gourmet entrees in five-star restaurants. The phrase "toys for big boys" is no longer just a chapter in a book on recreational therapy for the delusional. It is a badge. Of honor.

As a U.S. citizen, may I nominate a subject for a stamp that would do these same adults more good than Scooby-Doo? I nominate a street urchin who knew a cheater when he saw one and took the fight right to him.

What grown-up of today, sir, would confront a powerful insurance executive who had been cheating on a golf course and then threaten in unadorned language to spill the beans? Charles Bruckhauser did that at eleven years old.[†] That's all he did, but is it not enough?

I suggest that a picture of Charlie Bruckhauser should hang in a gold frame in the U.S. Senate. And on a stamp to remind the rest of us.

Little Charlie Bruckhauser was fearless. And why? Because no one ever gave him points for "gets along well with others." He wasn't disposed to that softy stuff, but he was at the ready to confront cheaters of any shape and size. If that meant that he'd be dragged before the board of trustees at the country club, that was fine with him, too. He didn't need a lawyer, a social worker, or God forbid, a parent to go with him. Charlie had power that nobody could take away: he knew a cheat when he saw one and he couldn't have cared less about getting along with the guy. If he happened to clear five clams in the process, so much the better.

---

‡   See chapter 5.

A few years ago, I happened to go to a baseball game at the University of Georgia, a regular-season game on a weekday afternoon. At my college, that would mean that in the unlikely event someone showed up to watch the game, they'd be handed a glove and asked to loosen up the pitchers. At UGA, we could barely get a parking space. The Bulldogs were playing the University of Mississippi, Ole Miss. As my relatives and I walked toward the stadium, I noticed a middle-aged man heading the same way, decked out in Bulldog clothes: hat, scarf, jacket, shirt, sweatpants, and foam hand. "Oooh," I murmured, "that poor man is disturbed. He should get a life." That was before I realized that most of the people in the crowd were middle-aged or a little older and except for the tiny Ole Miss contingent, they were *all* wearing black and red. All. (If one needed to exaggerate, one wouldn't tell the story.) Many were upholstered head to toe, just as was the first man I saw. After wondering where Margaret Mead was when one needed an anthropologist of primitive cultures, I settled in to watch the game.

I have seen ballgames live in every place where I could arrange it: big cities or tiny outposts. In every game—forgive me, in every other game—the fans appreciated a good play, even by the opposing team. Mostly, even in big playoff games in the major leagues, the crowd just sits there rather quietly, watching. At the game in Georgia, the crowd did have a life, a life of its own, united not so much in adoration of the Bulldogs but in searing, soaring hatred of the Ole Miss team. Every time the opposing pitcher threw a called strike, I heard noises all around that veritably retched the agony of the abused: the sound a yak would make when falling off a cliff. That was for a mere strike. Whenever a Bulldog player struck out, the cursing from my fellow fans was so vivid that I worried for the pitcher's safety. I worried for the future of the English language. I worried that I had been taken to a hockey game by mistake.

In all of the important ways—academics, architectural beauty, and landscaping—UGA is as good as any college in the country, but something strange happens when middle-aged people put on black and red there. It empowers them. They saw the UGA left fielder drop an easy "can of corn" pop fly, allowing the man on second to score, and they gave the finger—not the foam one—to the Ole Miss runner as he trotted into the dugout. It would not occur to anyone clad in basic Bulldog to criticize the clod playing left field. Never! When people are more than fans, more than loyal, they have branded themselves. If by some circumstance they are forced to admit that any being with whom they have branded themselves is unworthy, then they would have to unbrand themselves, a process as traumatic for a person with a dresser full of red and black knits as for a steer with the name of a ranch singed onto his rump. Self-branding effectively obviates accusations of cheating against the heroes of the brand.

Perhaps it is only slightly related, but my cousin Peter, a songwriter, was mildly obsessed with a sports team and nearing the point of having his judgment subsumed, as he was blinded and even branded by them. Down in the dumps after a bad loss one day, he looked up suddenly and said, "Does anybody on that team give a damn when I don't sell a song?" This was a profound advance, which instantly recaptured his sense of perspective. The fever thus broken, he reverted to being just a fan. After that, when his team did something wrong, he was the first to say they were overpaid, inept, broken-down, stuck-up losers.

FIG. 13.3—An Equation to Determine One's Ability to
Call a Cheater a Cheater[§]

PART I OF THE EQUATION

Please read the following background information first.

A. Alfred P. Sloan Jr. was a no-nonsense management expert who was largely responsible for organizing General Motors and then running it for almost fifty years. He was an honest dealer, but steely. As he walked into a tense negotiating session in the early 1950s, the room hushed. "He's a son of a bitch," murmured a GM executive standing nearby, "but he's our son of a bitch!"

B. My mother once toured the state for two months in a professional production of *Deathtrap*, which is a play about two writers tussling over a murder-mystery play who end up involved in a real-life murder mys-

---

§   *Please note: This applies only to bystanders. It is not for people at the time they have been directly cheated.*

tery. My ma was a seriously outstanding actress, but she wasn't a trouper. This was her one and only tour. The troupe of about ten players piled into a van together every few days, going to another small city, where they stayed at the same hotel and ate a few meals together, between performances. The leading man, who had never been married, got himself a girlfriend (*read:* love-slave) at each and every stop. The second leading man, who had been introduced to the company as a wonderfully married man with a new baby at home, did too. i.e., Did too get himself a love-slave at each and every stop.

C. Friends of mine were invited to a rather fabulous graduation party at a country club and were assigned seats of honor next to the father of the grad. Had I been invited, the hosts would have set up a table for one near the walk-in freezers. [*Sorry for that outburst. See chapter 7.*] At the graduation party, the conversation was general, until one of my friends asked that deeply probing question: "So what do you do for a living?" All the people mentioned were of the white race. The father of the grad explained that he had owned an appliance store and mentioned the location, which was an impoverished African American neighborhood. That would have been enough detail to satisfy my friends' polite curiosity about what this total

stranger did for a living, but the man continued in laboratory-level detail, boasting that
he'd became an expert at making sure black
people bought more than they could afford,
and if they didn't, then he took a different
tack, misleading them regarding the para-
meters of the transaction. When his customers thereupon missed payments, he took
back the appliances and later sold them
again—and again.

D. Frank Capra, the movie director, was literally going hungry on the street when he was
in his early twenties, a fact that is astonishing, since he was at the time a recent graduate of Caltech. As he related in his memoir,
he was penniless and malnourished. This
was during Prohibition days. The boss of
the organized crime mob in the region
heard about Capra's Caltech degree and offered him ten thousand dollars to design a
new still for making liquor. That figure was
roughly equivalent to a million dollars today.** Capra turned him down.

E. A person whose mother was an outstanding
actress...thinks up the plot of a play. It's

** The U.S. Bureau of Labor Statistics rates ten thousand 1920 dollars
as the equivalent of $132,000 today. In 1920, however, one could
buy a new house in a nice neighborhood for $2,000; one can't get
one today for $26,500. A super car such as the Mercer was $5,000
then; a similarly spectacular sports car today is about $500,000. In
other words, Capra could have bought five new houses or two new
Lamborghinis, if this happened today.

about a troupe that is touring the state—
in a play about two writers tussling over a
murder-mystery play who end up involved
in a real-life murder mystery—*and the two
leading men get love-slaves in every little town.*
Brilliant! What an original idea! After the
plot of the new play is mentioned in a
friendly way to an acquaintance in the
canasta league, said acquaintance absconds
with it, writes the play, and gets it produced.
The idea's originator opts against the conso-
lation prize: the chance to write a play about
two canasta players tussling over the idea
for a play—about a troupe that is touring
the state in a play about two writers tussling
over a murder-mystery play who end up involved in a real-life murder mystery...and
how the two leading men get love-slaves in
every little town.

PART II OF THE EQUATION

Now consult the matching letters, below and above,
and rate your inclination, from 1 to 4. Please think over
your answers carefully. There is no time limit.

Don't write in the book.

Scoring:

1 = Never. Ever.

2 = Circumstances would make this tempting, but...no.

3 = Doesn't seem quite right, but…yes.
4 = Sure. Why not?

Letter (See also above)	Question	Your rating
a.	Regarding someone who represents you as a leader—business, clerical, political, or other type—could you say the following sentence: "Sure he's a scrimy cheater…but he's *our* scrimy cheater!"	
b.	Some people in the acting troupe gave the second leading man the cold shoulder. Would you continue to socialize with him?	
c.	If you were in the position of my friends, would you keep mum, for the sake of the hosts, when the man told you about his business practices?	
d.	If you were in debt, with bills coming in fresh all the time, would you take the million dollars and work for cheaters?	
e.	If you were a mutual friend of the two canasta players, would you attend the Tony Awards?	
	Subtotal:	
	Divide by 5. This is your Turn-In-Cheaters (TIC) score:	

The lower your TIC score, the more you value integrity. The higher your rating, the more you have put one of those "something" factors above integrity in your priorities. But this is where the TIC score is especially revealing regarding the direction of change in the national character of America. A fair-to-middling score (2 or 3) doesn't reflect a person who places integrity second, but one who does allow that there are reasons someone else might do so. That, in effect, buffs the slippery slope that the nation is currently on. It gives no resistance to the trend that is under discussion, the de-emphasis of the virtue in "public virtue." Ominously, that trend continues to erase the overriding fact that a non-cheater is not merely the practicioner but the guardian of integrity. When those who still perceive the line start to let sham dealing wash over it for some reason, for any reason, then we can say with perfect historical accuracy that George Washington was wasting his time with his Four Pillars. And that the "citty upon a hill" turned out close up to be a sign for the exit. Such is the specter that worries the realist, transfixed by the slumping national character, and delights the cynic.

For the master cynic, it is sometimes amusing to think about the world a hundred years from now. To wonder idly if the cardboard boxes in one's basement will be unpacked by then. Probably not. Past that, the master of cynicism takes comfort in the certain knowledge that everything will be just as cruddy as ever in the early twenty-second century, let's face it. Or nearly everything. There are, after all, times when pessimism is a luxury.

If we are looking forward at the people in the 2100s, they will just as certainly be looking back in time at us.

"A hundred years ago," the little kids will ask in that future day, "everything was really cruddy, wasn't it?"

Smart kids.

"Yes, it truly was," the teacher will say. "Except that Americans in the early 2000s did one really heroic thing for this country."

"What did they do?" the little kids will ask.

"They finally heard what George Washington was trying to tell them."

Afterword

O h, hurrah! Oh, hurrah! Oh, hurrah!" said everyone even the kittens.

Acknowledgments

The first formal interview conducted for this research was with my neighbor, Quentin Rogers, one of my best friends, I'm proud to say. He arrived on time, a little bit dressed up, and sat in my living room answering questions while I took notes on a clipboard. Quentin told me a story of cheating so gripping and absolutely astonishing, about his third-grade classmates and their teacher, that I knew at once it would blow the top off of American education today. His mother was sitting a little way off, listening too. On the way out, she took me aside. "He made that story up," she said with a smile. "He wanted so much to help you with your book." And so he did.

My brother Philip and my great friend Kevin S. Quinn each sent along ideas on cheating, which I was always glad to see.

Samantha Deming, MA, LMFT, has a rare ability to pinpoint the vortex of problems in relationships. Her experience is very much in that field, since she sees predominantly couples in her family therapy practice in two communities in greater Los Angeles, Santa Clarita and Encino. Samantha is also an adjunct professor in psychology at Pepperdine University in Malibu. She was wonderfully generous to this project, granting permission to use her material on identifying chronic marital cheaters (see Chapter 11).

Sharon Gissy of the Chicago Public Library very gracefully came to the rescue in my search for a usable image of Charlie Bruckhauser, and I'm indebted to her. Dawn Bonner at Mount Vernon kindly helped with the photograph of George Washington. It depicts Jean-Antoine Houdon's 1785 bust of the founder, made from life. The piece was transferred to the Mount Vernon Ladies' Association through the generosity of John Augustine Washington III in 1860.

In the midst of writing the book, we had a death in our family, the kind of disaster that makes one lose interest in anything more complicated than mowing the lawn. After a span of that, I had an idea. I decided to buy a classic sports car, in order to have fun again. It is through that action that I can report that a person in a hurry to buy a sports car attracts many more cheaters than a person writing a book on such people. Knocking from one crooked deal and con job to another, I was about to give up and go back to my lawn mowing when I found a yellow convertible being sold by Ron Brook of New Jersey. I treasure the car, which is in my garage as I write this, but not nearly as much as all of the enthusiasm, humor, and kindness that Ron sent my way with his "baby." What a difference he made, as he patiently explained for the fifth and then the sixth time how to tune the carburetors and then listened to my plans for this book. He also contributed one of the most significant stories herein (see Chapter 2).

The following people nagged, cajoled, or scolded me into finishing my work on *Cheaters Always Win*, for which I am grateful: my agent, Julia Lord, Paul Birchmeyer, Matt Callaway, Nancy Gaskill, Jeffrey Tuck, Douglas Brinkley, Rachel Kambury, Jill Olmsted, D.D. and Beverly Fenster, Tim Fenster, and Peter and Diane Berk.

The following person did not, for which I am even more grateful: Sean Desmond, the publisher and editor of the book. Moreover, he was instrumental in shaping the project and the potential that it offered to a fortunate author.

Notes

INTRODUCTION

xviii **his place as the first admitted:** Donald J. Trump with Kate Bohner, *The Art of the Comeback* (New York: Times Books, 1997), p. 116.

1. YOUR OWN KIND

5 **apparel, brings in $13 million per year:** Michael Casagrande, "Alabama Athletics Brings in School Record $177 Million Revenue, Profits Dip," AL.com, January 16, 2019.

5 **"I happen to know for a fact:** Sheila John Daly, "Teen Mail," *Longview* (Texas) *News-Journal,* April 6, 1969, p. 55.

11 **"I saw one of his," Seminick reported:** Frank Dolson, "Doctoring Is No Recent Phenomenon," *Philadelphia Inquirer,* August 9, 1987, pp. 1E, 6E.

11 **Such examples were commonly traded:** Chris Baker, "Perry Kept Catcher in the Dark," *Los Angeles Times,* August 25, 1982, part III. p. 1.

12 **he was finally tossed from a game:** "Perry Fined, Suspended for 10

Days," Associated Press, *Los Angeles Times,* August 25, 1982, part III. p. 1.

12 **titling his 1974 book:** Gaylord Perry with Bob Sudyk, *Me and the Spitter: An Autobiographical Confession* (New York: Saturday Review Press, 1974).

13 **Louis DiGiulio was a wiseguy in Rochester:** Jody McPhillips, "Defense Attacks Star Witness in Mob-Murder Trial," *Rochester (N.Y.) Democrat and Chronicle,* November 19, 1983, p. 2.

2. TO BE OR NOT TO CHEAT

17 **"What are the ring names of the four":** "Pugilism and History Figure in Quiz Show," *Chicago Tribune,* November 16, 1955, p. 42.

18 **An impoverished poet from Greenwich Village:** Richard N. Goodwin, *Remembering America: A Voice from the Sixties* (New York: Open Road Integrated Media, 2014), p. 53.

19 **their categories against "type":** "The $60 Million Question," *TIME,* April 22, 1957, p. 96.

20 **knew the name of the canals:** "St. Louisan Bests Two Experts, Boosts TV Winnings to $88,000," *St. Louis Post-Dispatch,* March 11, 1957, p. 7. This incident, which involved a champion player named Theodore Nadler, occurred on the adjunct program, *$64,000 Challenge.*

21 **The producers were less than pleased:** William V. Thomas, "Dr. Joyce Brothers: A Nation Cries on Her Shoulder," *Baltimore Sun,* p. E10.

22 **she answered a six-part question:** "Here Is Quiz Which Won $64,000; Girl Expert Answers Queries," *San Francisco Examiner,* December 7, 1955, p. 10.

23 **For six hours, she batted:** Betty Parham, "Q&A on the News," *Atlanta Constitution,* September 30, 1994, p. 2.

23 **"The grand jury asked me boxing questions:** Thomas, "Dr. Joyce Brothers: A Nation Cries on Her Shoulder."

25 **"My wife knows how to press":** Lewis Yablonsky, *The Extra-Sex Factor* (New York: New York Times Books, 1979), p. 17.

26 **the city's kosher inspector, Frank Brickman:** "Miami Beach's 'Kosher Cop' Butchers' Terror," *Palm Beach Post,* May 1, 1977, p. 39.

26 **a delicate yellow cake:** Lord Frederick Hamilton, *Vanished Pomps of Yesterday* (New York: George Doran, 1921), pp 109–10. Lord Frederick's story was paraphrased.

28 **"So nobody ate meat that night":** "Miami Beach's 'Kosher Cop' Butchers' Terror."

28 **described by a colleague as "a walking event":** Brian Williams, quoted in "Sheela Allen-Stephens, Former NBC 10 Reporter, Dies," *Philadelphia Tribune,* October 24, 2016, p. 1.

28 **"I had seventy-five signals":** Dave Bittan, "A Look at Local Cheating," *Philadelphia Daily News,* August 31, 1983, p. 29.

29 **four-year-old Ron Brook frequently walked:** Author interviews, August 2018.

31 **retired people who spent money:** Clint H. Denman, "Justice in Economic Life," King City (Missouri) *Tri-County News,* September 12, 1958, p. 2.

31 **looking intently through his microscope:** Ron Rapoport, "'Dear Mom' Wasn't the Right Answer," *Minneapolis Star,* January 28, 1965, p. 46.

3. POWER PLAY

33 **Way down in the bottom:** Lydia Parrish, *Slave Songs of the Georgia Sea Islands* (Athens, Georgia: Brown Thrasher Books, 1992), pp. 247–48.

34 **"never took a dollar":** "'Yellow Kid,' master swindler who made millions, dies at 100," *Chicago Tribune,* February 27, 1976, p. 3.

34 **the Yellow Kid asked an acquaintance:** "The Yellow Kid Beats $3 Case by Technicality," *Chicago Daily Tribune,* December 10, 1949, p. 11.

34 **he solicited funds from wealthy:** "Yellow Kid Weil in Cell Has Hand Out for Money," *Chicago Tribune,* March 21, 1928, p. 14.

35 **"You have to be blind":** Hilda Jackson, "Cheating the Blind," *The New York Times,* May 15, 1921, p. 98.

39 **In a letter of 1803:** Thomas Jefferson to William Henry Harrison, February 27, 1803, in Albert Ellery Bergh and Andrew A Lipscomb, editors, *The Writings of Thomas Jefferson,* vol. 10 (Washington, D.C.: Thomas Jefferson Memorial Association, 1903), pp. 369–71.

40 **bought a huge, isolated tract:** Louis F. Burns, *A History of the Osage People* (University of Alabama Press, 2009), p. 344.

42 **by emergency Federal legislation:** *The Osage People and Their Trust Property: A Field Report* (Anadarko Area Office, Bureau of Indian Affairs, 1953). p. 63.

42 **worked out to 93 percent:** Molly Stephey, "The Osage Murders: Oil, Wealth and the FBI's First Big Case," National Museum of the American Indian, blogpost, March 1, 2011.

42 **"the largest gatherer of crude oil":** Charles G. Koch, *Good Profit: How Creating Value for Others Built One of the World's Most Successful Companies* (New York: Crown Business, 2015), p. 90.

43 **single biggest purchaser of oil:** *A Report of the Special Committee on Investigations of the Select Committee on Indian Affairs. Senate, 101st Congress, 1st Session* (Washington: U.S. Government Printing Office, November 20, 1989), p. 12.

43 **other companies, including Conoco:** *A Report of the Special Committee,* p.107.

43 **Koch Industries used a special system:** Ibid., pp. 106, 109.

43 **In one year, 1985:** Russell Ray, "Jury Finds Koch Cheated," *Tulsa World,* December 24, 1999, p. 1.

43 **One might also argue, as Koch did:** Koch, *Good Profit,* p. 90.

43 **Koch estimates were invariably found:** *A Report of the Special Committee,* p. 106.

44 **Pale Moon sang the "Star Spangled Banner":** "Moon Also Rises," *Dayton Journal Herald,* July 18, 1980, p. 4.

44 **"Pale Moon" was a fraud:** "U.S. Furor Mars Spain's Expo '92," Associated Press, *Pittsburgh Post-Gazette,* April 21, 1992, p. 3; "Eagles Were Tested for AIDS," *Chicago Tribune,* November 1, 1991, p. 56; Jack Anderson, "Knife Fiasco Cuts Credibility," Danville (Pennsylvania) *News,* July 1, 1997, p. 4.

44 **representing Indian causes:** Sean Schultz, "Look Inward for Beauty, Speaker Says," *Green Bay Press-Gazette,* July 7, 1987, p. 27; Mike Sager, "Princess Pale Moon at the Edge of the Spotlight," *Washington Post,* May 2, 1982, p. 11.

44 **Jamake Highwater, another fake Cherokee:** Rachel Howard, "Indian Giver," *San Francisco Examiner,* July 15, 2001, p. C1; Kathryn Shanley, "The Indians America Loves to Love and Read," in *Native*

American Representations: First Encounters, Distorted Images and Literary Appropriations, edited by Gretchen M. Bataille (Lincoln: University of Nebraska, 2001), pp. 32–38; Jack Anderson, "This 'Indian' Speaking with Forked Tongue?" *Philadelphia Daily News,* February 16, 1984, p. 54.

44 **Elizabeth Warren was presenting herself:** Michael Levenson, "Warren Makes Case with DNA Results," *Boston Globe,* October 16, 2018, pp. 1, 4.

44 **her background traced genetically:** Victoria McGrane, "Warren Defends Timing of DNA Test's Release," *Boston Globe,* October 17, 2018, p. A1.

45 **a professor at the University of California–Riverside:** Scott Jaschik, "Fake Cherokee?" *Inside Higher Ed*, July 6, 2015.

45 **Native American studies at Dartmouth:** "Dartmouth College Native American Director of the Job," *Burlington Free Press,* October 2, 2015, p. A12.

46 **intervention from Senator Bob Dole and other:** Phillip L. Zweig and Michael Schroeder, "Bob Dole's Oil Patch Pals," *Bloomberg*, April 1, 1996.

46 **His contention was that:** Leslie Wayne, "Brother Versus Brother; Koch Family's Long Legal Feud Is Headed for a Jury," *The New York Times,* April 28, 1999.

46 **"The Osage," said Bill Koch's attorney:** Ray, "Jury Finds Koch Cheated," p. 1.

46 **In hockey terms:** For a discussion of the good intentions and checkered results of federal law relating to the cheating of Indian oil businesses, see Kent Siegrist, "Honor Among Thieves: The Absence of Adequate Enforcement Protections for Native American Royalty Theft," *American Indian Law Review,* 30–1, 2005/2006, pp. 223–45.

47 **Outside companies forced many:** Lauren Donovan, "Adrift in a Flood of Work," *Bismarck Tribune,* March 9, 2014, p. 1.

47 **he fathered a baby with Hall's teenaged:** Deborah Sontag and Brent McDonald, "Where Oil, Corruption and Bodies Surface," *The New York Times,* December 29, 2014, p. 1.

4. ROOKED BUT GOOD

50 **"This chapter was a small but painful part"**: William Neikirk and Mike Dorning, "GOP Won't Let Debate Be Delayed," *Chicago Tribune,* December 18, 1998, p. 27.

50 **"The remorse I feel will always"**: Stephanie Gaskell and Bill Hutchinson, "I'm No Monster Sez N.J. Gal Who Brought Down the Gov.," *Daily News,* March 13, 2008, p. 5.

50 **"I would secondly say to [my wife]"**: Ron Barnett, "Jenny Sanford Asked for Separation," *Greenville News,* June 25, 2009, p. 9.

50 **"I want to thank my colleagues"**: Celeste Katz, "Anthony Weiner's Short Goodbye: Transcript," June 16, 2011.

52 **"I wish I were independent"**: Ruth Alden, "'Just a Wife' Tells 'Undecided' to Leave Cheating Husband," *Detroit Free Press,* April 13, 1932, p. 9.

55 **In 1977, a woman calling herself**: Ann Landers, "How Lies Can Hurt Innocent People," *Philadelphia Inquirer,* November 22, 1977, p. 23.

55 **The advice of forbearance and turning a blind eye**: Ann Landers, "Figure Is Good But Nose Problem," *Ottawa Journal,* March 26, 1965, p. 26. In typical advice, she wrote, "The cheating husband is insecure and needs to keep proving himself. And the wise wife understands this."

56 **Landers considered that she**: Carol Felsenthal, "Dear Ann," *Chicago Magazine,* February 1, 2003.

57 **woman with twelve children at home**: "Mother of Ten Is Accused," *Philadelphia Inquirer,* March 17, 1917, p. 14.

58 ***Cheating Cheaters* was first staged**: "Too Many Crooks Spoil No Broth; 'Cheating Cheaters' Proves to Be Exciting and Also Amusing," *New York Tribune,* August 10, 1916, p. 7; "Community Events," Newport News (Virginia) *Daily Press,* January 16, 2003, p. D7.

59 **A young writer who knew Marcin**: Frederica Sagor Maas, *The Shocking Miss Pilgrim: A Writer in Early Hollywood* (Lexington: University Press of Kentucky, 1999), p. 76.

59 **win "a $10,000 short story contest"**: Martin Kane, "Broadway," *Pittsburgh Press,* January 28, 1943, p. 13.

59 **he came in eighth:** "The $10,000 Prize Winners," *Buffalo Courier,* May 19, 1912, p. 14.

60 **When Ongley came up with an outline:** "'Cheating Cheaters' Cheat Is Charged," *Pittsburgh Daily Post,* February 21, 1917, p. 10.

60 **Ongley had fallen out the window:** "Plunges to Death from Hotel Window," Wilmington (Delaware) *Morning News,* October 25, 1915, p. 2.

61 **pulling together a living for herself:** "Stone Opera House," *Binghamton Press and Sun-Bulletin,* October 15, 1920, p. 15.

61 **took her case:** "Victory for Max Marcin," Brooklyn *Daily Eagle,* June 1, 1917, p. 9.

61 **"suave and cool" Brooklyn lawyer:** Mary Hosie, "Two Follow Footsteps of Successful Fathers," Brooklyn *Eagle,* August 18, 1940, p. 4; "Vanderbilt Weds Miss Littleton," *New York Herald,* April 30, 1920, p. 4.

62 **"the town's foremost criminal lawyers":** Richard Massock, "Nathan Burkan, Actor's Friend," *Gettysburg Times,* May 7, 1930, p. 4.

62 ***Ongley v. Marcin* for example:** *Ongley v. Marcin et al.,* 180 App. Div. 685, Supreme Court, First Department, 1917; *Ongley v. Marcin,* 214 App. Div. 455 (N.Y. App. Div 1925).

62 **In 1927, it was over:** "Woods' Riches Cited in Pleas to Court," *The New York Times,* June 3, 1927, p. 25.

62 **in 1929, it was over again***: Losch v. Marcin,* 251 N.Y. 402 (N.Y. 1929). After Amy Ongley died in 1926, her mother, Fidelia S. Losch, took over as executrix of the estate and plaintiff in the case. See "Wills for Probate," *The New York Times,* December 30, 1926, p. 38.

64 **At Syracuse University in upstate New York:** "Walk out of Class on Cheaters," *Orlando Sentinel,* February 19, 1933, p. 2.

5. GAME CHANGE

68 **When a caddy, noted the paper:** "The Blackmailing Caddie," Brooklyn *Eagle,* September 1, 1922, p. 4.

69 **"Caddies have been a nuisance":** "Caddy Incites 'Revolution' in Golf Club," *Chicago Tribune,* August 30, 1922, p. 1.

69 **the dominant New York Insurance Company:** "Directors Put in Entire Control of the Corporation," *The New York Times,* January 4, 1907, p. 14.

69 **the North American Insurance Company:** "Love for Actress Led Boy to Theft," *Buffalo Times,* March 2, 1917, p. 11. Kent had his problems with young people: According to this article, he cut his twenty-year-old son off without a penny and then tried to have him incarcerated when the young man dropped everything to follow a particular chorus girl all over the country.

70 **The penalty was suspension:** "Golf Card Scandal Stirs Chicago Club," *New York Herald,* August 31, 1922, p. 14.

70 **a player from Galveston, Texas:** Orlando Blackburn, "List of Cheater's Tricks," Galveston *Daily News,* November 12, 1983, p. 19.

74 **"We were just trying to get":** Larry Woody, "Gainin' an Edge," Nashville *Tennessean,* July 6, 1986, p. 6-C.

74 **"In other parts of the country":** Warner Hessler, "NBA Needs Image Assist from Samson," Newport News *Daily Press,* October 12, 1983, p. 22.

75 **Smokey Yunick had equipped his Pontiac:** Woody, "Gainin' an Edge."

75 **Fred Lorenzen, a prominent driver:** Jerry Garrett, "Marcis, Penske Team Avoids Talladega Scandal," Orangeburg (South Carolina) *Times and Democrat,* August 7, 1977, p. 16.

75 **Weight regulations in NASCAR races:** Woody, "Gainin' an Edge."

76 **a woman in Las Vegas used to wander:** Mario Puzo, "When the Chips Are Down," Pittsburgh *Press Roto,* May 1, 1977, p. 18.

78 **"You've got to cheat to win in NASCAR:** Woody, "Gainin' an Edge."

79 **"It was a very gray area":** Garrett, "Marcis, Penske Team Avoids Talladega Scandal."

80 **"Gramma will either be out back":** Marilyn Montgomery, "Not in the Cards," Lebanon (Oregon) *Express,* August 16, 1979, p. 11.

7. YOUR OWN KIND

91 **celebrated her tenth wedding anniversary:** Laura Kavesh and Cheryl Lavin, "A Relationship Born of Cheating Dies of Cheating," *Chicago Tribune,* June 18, 1986, p. 56.

99 **a Harvard boy walked by a man:** Heywood Broun, "Good for the Soul," *Pittsburgh Press,* May 8, 1930, p. 2.

101 **When a pair of men's Bible classes:** "Bible Classes Drop Disputes," Miami (Florida) *News,* November 13, 1923, p. 1.

104 **After Richard Nixon was:** Richard Nixon, *RN: The Memoirs of Richard Nixon* (New York: Simon & Schuster, 1978).

104 **Tony Graziano of Canastota:** Author interview.

105 **He was an old friend of MacDougall's:** Mickey MacDougall, "They Never Give the Sucker a Break," *Pittsburgh Sun-Telegraph,* September 26, 1943, p. 56.

8. TO CHEAT OR NOT TO BE

109 **A Midwesterner named Itchy Novak:** Herb Michelson, "Here's One Way to Get That 'A,'" *Akron Beacon Journal,* May 11, 1958, p. 1D.

112 **Pasteur didn't flinch:** Gerald L. Geison, *The Private Science of Louis Pasteur* (Princeton: Princeton University Press), pp. 238–39.

113 **the work of a veterinary scientist:** Patrice Debré, *Louis Pasteur* (Baltimore: The Johns Hopkins University Press, 1998), p. 396.

113 **"He would do anything to pull off":** Robert E. Kohler, "Reviewed Work: The Private Science of Louis Pasteur," *Isis,* 87–2, June 1996, p. 332.

114 **"I wish to my God he would bite":** John Ireland, *Letters and Poems by the Late Mr. John Henderson with Anecdotes of His Life* (London: J. Johnson, 1786), p. 60.

114 **"persons who attend the movies":** Hugh Hartshorne and Mark A. May, *Studies in Deceit* (New York: Macmillan, 1930).

116 **she was disqualified from both races:** Tony Burton, "Suspicion Grows That Rose Is Full of Thorns," *New York Daily News,* April 24, 1980, p. C3; John Powers, "Ruiz Ruled Out—Gareau Is In," *Boston Globe,* April 30, 1980, p. 69.

116 **One poor man in Hawaii:** Scott Ostler, "Cheaters Don't Win, but They Often Run," Santa Rosa *Press-Democrat,* March 7, 1986, p. 23.

117 **"I might fudge on my taxes":** Ibid.

118 **the authors of the study:** Raymond Philip Morris, "Hugh Hartshorne, 1885–1967," *Religious Education,* vol. 63, no. 3, 1968, p. 162; "College Student Should Not Be Required to Pay Tuition Back to Parents," Olean (New York) *Times-Herald,* March 24, 1924, p. 25.

118 **Harry Baker in Detroit:** "Can't Spell? You're Not So Dumb at That," Rhinelander (Wisconsin) *Daily News,* December 28, 1929, p. 3.

119 **"Cheaters," two professors there wrote:** "Pampering by Mama Helps Make Cheats?" *Cincinnati Enquirer,* February 21, 1965, p. 15H.

119 **A study in New Jersey:** "School Cheats' Folks Blamed," *New York Daily News,* January 31, 1969, p. 6.

119 **An economist at Yale with a macroeconomic:** Ray C. Fair, "A Theory of Extramarital Affairs," *Journal of Political Economy,* vol. 86, no. 1, February 1978, pp. 45–60.

122 **A recent experiment departed:** C. Daniel Batson, Elizabeth R. Thompson, Greg Seuferling, Heather Whitney, and Jon A. Strongman, "Moral Hypocrisy: Appearing Moral to Oneself Without Being So," *Journal of Personality and Social Psychology,* 77–3, 1999, pp. 526–534.

122 **"The best business in Juarez":** "Juarez Tourists Given Warning," Longview (Texas) *News-Journal,* August 13, 1969, p. 20.

123 **"I got tired of losing":** Fred Rothenberg, "In the Recruiting Game, Cheaters Can Be Winners," *Cincinnati Enquirer,* January 1, 1979, D-3.

123 **Moses Annenberg, known as "Moe":** "Colossal Cheat," *Elmira Star-Gazette,* July 5, 1940, p. 6.

9. POWER PLAY

128 **Cooperative Institutional Research Program: 1967:** Robert J. Panos, Alexander W. Astin, and John A. Creager, *National Norms for Entering Freshmen—Fall 1967* (Washington: American Council on Education Research Reports, 1967), vol. 2, No. 7, p. 34; **1973:** Alexander W. Astin, Margo R. King, John M. Light, and Gerald T. Richardson, *National Norms for Entering Freshmen—Fall 1973* (Los

Angeles: Cooperative Institutional Research Program, 1973), p. 37; **1976:** Alexander W. Astin, Margo R. King, and Gerald T. Richardson, *National Norms for Entering Freshmen—Fall 1976* (Los Angeles: Cooperative Institutional Research Program, 1976), p. 32; **1986:** Alexander W. Astin, Kenneth C. Green, William S. Korn, and Marilynn Schalit, *The American Freshman: National Norms for Fall 1986* (Los Angeles: Cooperative Institutional Research Program, 1986), p. 64; **1992:** Eric L. Day, Alexander W. Astin, William S. Korn, and Ellyne R. Riggs, *The American Freshman: National Norms for Fall 1992* (Los Angeles: Cooperative Institutional Research Program, 1992), p. 25; **1996:** Linda J. Sax, Alexander W. Astin, William S. Korn, and Kathryn M. Mahoney, *The American Freshman: National Norms for Fall 1996* (Los Angeles: Cooperative Institutional Research Program, 1996), p. 27; **2006:** John H. Pryor, Sylvia Hurtado, Victor B. Saenz, Jessica S. Korn, José Luis Santos, and William S. Korn, *The American Freshman: National Norms for Fall 2006* (Los Angeles: Cooperative Institutional Research Program, 2006), p. 39; **2014:** Kevin Eagan, Ellen Bara Stolzenberg, Joseph J. Ramirez, Melissa C. Aragon, Maria Ramirez Suchard, and Sylvia Hurtado, *The American Freshman: National Norms Fall 2014* (Los Angeles: Cooperative Institutional Research Program, 2014), p. 44; **2016:** Kevin Eagan, Ellen Bara Stolzenberg, Hilary B. Zimmerman, Melissa C. Aragon, Hannah Whang Sayson, and Cecilia Rios-Agular, *The American Freshman: National Norms Fall 2016* (Los Angeles: Cooperative Institutional Research Program, 2016), p. 47.

131 **There is no mystery in business:** John D. Rockefeller, *Random Reminiscences of Men and Events* (Garden City, New York: Doubleday, Doran & Company, 1909), p. 132.

135 **"My boy didn't cheat—he just":** Will Grimsley, "A Question of Honor," *Miami News,* January 31, 1965, p. 19.

135 **"We sent our boy to the academy":** Ibid.

135 **"We, the citizens, should thank":** Richard F. Boyce, letter, *Albuquerque Journal,* February 5, 1965, p. 5.

136 **"Here's my excuse":** Lisa Miller, "Ethical Parenting: Is There Such a Thing? Ask Your Children," *New York Magazine,* 46–30, October 14, 2013, p. 28.

136 **a biology teacher in the small town:** Clayton Bellamy, "Teacher's Plight Renews Call for Honesty," Springfield (Missouri) *News-Leader*, February 7, 2002, p. 10.

137 **The high school principal looked:** "In Kansas, OK to Cheat," Springfield (Missouri) *News-Leader*, February 9, 2002, p. 12.

137 **At a meeting on December 11, the board:** "Teacher Quits after Grades Changed," Manhattan (Kansas) *Mercury*, January 31, 2002, p. A3.

137 **In another vote, five months:** "Board upholds plagiarism decision," Manhattan (Kansas) *Mercury*, April 3, 2002, p. A3.

138 **"all the more amazing because":** "An Image Shattered," *Des Moines Tribune*, May 29, 1965, p. 6.

138 **One of the Americans noticed:** Alan Truscott, "Why 10 Charged Bridge Cheating," *The New York Times*, May 27, 1965, p. 34.

139 **the ways that Reese and Schapiro:** Marshall Smith, "A Cheating Scandal Rocks the Bridge World," *LIFE*, June 4, 1965, pp. 32–33.

140 **"The hypothesis was checked against 17 deals":** Truscott, "Why 10 Charged Bridge Cheating."

140 **"I had no difficulty," Reese later wrote:** Terence Reese, *Story of an Accusation* (London: Chess & Bridge Limited, 2004), p. 126.

141 **one of his colleagues announced:** Duncan Gordham and Patrick Jourdain, "Bridge Cheat 'Confession' after 40 Years," *London Telegraph*, May 10, 2005.

10. ROOKED BUT GOOD

145 **"I had about three dollars":** Bill Beeney, "The Lawyer Had a Losing Case," Rochester *Democrat and Chronicle*, January 14, 1965, p. 26.

148 **a Missouri man named Ed Bryson:** Ronald Koziol, "Success of a Credit Card Cheat," *Chicago Tribune*, February 11, 1972, p. 3; "They Couldn't Buy Off Credit Card Cheater," Troy (New York) *Record*, February 12, 1972, p. 1.

151 **perpetrated by a college professor:** Patricia Marby Harrison, "'Culture of Cheating' Threatens to Erode Learning Environment," Greenville (South Carolina) *News*, February 26, 2001, p. 7.

151 "And as I go into teaching": Barbara Shumway, "Details, Monotony Generate Cheating," Phoenix *Arizona Republic,* January 10, 1969, p. 53.

152 the mother at a parent-teacher conference: Judy White, "Rap Session," Mount Carmel (Illinois) *Daily Republican-Register,* March 30, 1972, p. 13.

153 presented a study of Shakespeare's: Harrison, "'Culture of Cheating' Threatens to Erode Learning Environment."

153 man by the name of Randy: Jack and Michael Strauss, "A Friendly Fraud," *Pittsburgh Press,* April 19, 1965, p. 45.

11. GAME CHANGE

159 "A man who will consent": "Base Ball," Brooklyn *Eagle,* February 5, 1877, p. 3.

160 placing ads in various columns: Advertisement, Seibert & McCloud, *New York Daily Herald,* June 24, 1874, p. 1.

160 "Buy Bertram to win in 3 innings": "Caught at Last," *New York Daily Herald,* July 23, 1876, p. 5.

161 Devlin flatly rejected Seibert's: "The Full Confessions of Hall and Devlin; How Those Innocent Lambs Were Led Astray," *Chicago Tribune,* November 4, 1877, p. 7.

162 "to strike an effective blow": William Hulbert to Bob Ferguson, 1877, quoted in Michael Haupert, "William Hulbert and the Birth of the National League," *Baseball Research Journal,* Spring 2015.

163 If you Can do me this favor: James Devlin to Harry Wright, 1878, quoted in ibid.

164 The outer door opened and: Albert Goodwill Spalding, *America's National Game* (New York: American Sports Publishers, 1911), p. 228.

166 In a recent Super Bowl: Adam Kilgore, "Julian Edelman began the season with a PED suspension and ended it as Super Bowl MVP," *Washington Post,* February 4, 2019.

168 75 percent "Don't know": "75 Percent of Oklahoma High School Students Can't Name the First President of the U.S." News 9

(Oklahoma City), October 6, 2009. According to the report, "The survey was commissioned by the Oklahoma Council of Public Affairs." To be technical, only 23 percent of the high schoolers named Washington.

168 **A woman in Missouri:** "Cry on Geraldine's Shoulder," *Oakland Tribune,* June 17, 1930, p. 33.

170 **Was your spouse with someone else:** Samantha Deming and Victor Deming, "Second Chances: Not All Cheaters Cheat Again," Santa Clarita (California) *Signal,* February 27, 2000, p. 14. The questions and indicated analysis are from the cited article.

171 **"For a marriage to work":** Dahleen Glanton, Couples Tie Tighter Knots in 'Covenant' Marriage," *Chicago Tribune,* January 2, 2005, p. 1.

173 **"has heard nothing of the over-emphasis":** Red Newton, "Proctor, Captain-Elect of Gators, Says Jenkins and Osgood are Slated for Line," *Tampa Tribune,* January 27, 1931, p. 9.

174 **Proctor had been caught cheating:** "C. Proctor of Tampa Expelled from State U.," *Tampa Tribune,* March 14, 1931, p. 1.

174 **"What, under Heaven, was the need":** Francis Bellamy, letter, *Tampa Tribune,* March 16, 1931, p. 4.

175 **"He is old enough to know":** "Mrs. B.," letter, *Tampa Tribune,* March 24, 1931, p. 4.

175 **Another woman, Janet Sellars:** Janet Sellars, letter, *Tampa Tribune,* March 29, 1931, p. 6.

177 **"a pilgrim, kicked by fate":** Red Newton, "The Morning After," *Tampa Tribune,* August 21, 1932, p. 9.

12. SECTION TWO CONCLUSION

179 **"One Has My Name" was a hit:** "Western Disc Hits," advertisement, Bush Radio & Appliance, Atchison (Kansas) *Daily Globe,* October 1, 1948, p. 2. "One Has My Name, the Other Has My Heart" was the number-one record. To give an idea of the unusual nature of that subject matter for a Western song at the time, the next three songs were "Dog House Boogie," "Starlight Waltz," and "Lost John Boogie."

179 **the Kendalls, made a career:** J. Garland Pembroke, "The Kendalls Cheated Their Way to the Top in Sound Style," *Atlanta Constitution Weekend,* March 15, 1986, p. 20.

180 **"The station will get a lot":** Jack Roberts, "Country Music Enough to Make Your Ears Blush," *Miami News,* February 9, 1979, p. 5.

181 **In the late 1970s, Reggie Carter:** Fred Rothenberg, "Hawaii's Reggie Carter Caper," *Honolulu Star-Bulletin,* December 19, 1978, p. 37.

13. YOUR AMERICA TODAY

188 **"as in all times some must be":** John Winthrop, *A Modell of Christian Charity, Massachusetts Historical Society Collections* (Boston: Massachusetts Historical Society, 1838), pp. 31–48.

193 **universal practice has in a measure legalized it:** Albert Brisbane, *Social Destiny of Man* (Philadelphia: C. F. Stollmeyer, 1840), p. 305.

193 **"When it was small enough not":** Alexandra Ossola, "The Web is still in its awkward teenage phase according to its father, Tim Berners-Lee," *Quartz,* March 12, 2019, https://qz.com/1568970.

197 **Three little kittens lost:** William J. Bennet, editor, *Book of Virtues* (New York: Simon & Schuster, 1993), pp. 188–89.

199 **"By furtively indulging":** Joshua Green, "The Bookie of Virtue," *Washington Monthly,* June 2003.

200 **become a "national scold":** Ian Mylchreest, "Casinos' Conduct in Question about Bennett Disclosures," *Las Vegas Business Press,* May 12, 2003, p. 3.

Index